RETIREMENT

BUILT

—— TO ——

LAST

T0165686

RETIREMENT

BUILT
—— TO ——
LAST

PLANNING FOR WHEN THE

PAYCHECKS STOP

DANIEL S. MILLER, CFP®

Published by Advantage, Charleston, South Carolina.
Member of Advantage Media Group.

ADVANTAGE is a registered trademark, and the Advantage colophon is a trademark of Advantage Media Group, Inc.

Printed in the United States of America.

ISBN: 978-1-59932-696-2
LCCN: 2016934281

Book design by Katie Biondo.

This publication is designed to provide accurate and authoritative information in regard to the subject matter covered. It is sold with the understanding that the publisher is not engaged in rendering legal, accounting, or other professional services. If legal advice or other expert assistance is required, the services of a competent professional person should be sought.

Advantage Media Group is proud to be a part of the Tree Neutral® program. Tree Neutral offsets the number of trees consumed in the production and printing of this book by taking proactive steps such as planting trees in direct proportion to the number of trees used to print books. To learn more about Tree Neutral, please visit www.treeneutral.com. To learn more about Advantage's commitment to being a responsible steward of the environment, please visit www.advantagefamily.com/green

Advantage Media Group is a publisher of business, self-improvement, and professional development books and online learning. We help entrepreneurs, business leaders, and professionals share their Stories, Passion, and Knowledge to help others Learn & Grow. Do you have a manuscript or book idea that you would like us to consider for publishing? Please visit advantagefamily.com or call 1.866.775.1696.

To my father, Max Miller.
Thanks for teaching me to be a good father, to always do the right thing, and to be good to people whenever you can.

Acknowledgments

To my wife, Denise Miller. Without her love and support for our life together and this crazy business we are in, I don't know where we would be today. She has been there through the good and the bad and has always believed in what we were striving to achieve. I could not ask for a better partner in business or in life. To her and our kids, Jackson and Andrea, I owe everything.

To my brother and best friend, Steve Miller. Steve is the one person who has always been in my corner no matter what the situation or obstacle in front of me. I owe much to him for his guidance as an older brother over the years. Along with our father, he has always shown me the value of hard work. He was my original business partner as a young man, and I'm proud to say that relationship still exists today.

To my mother and father-in-law Darrell and Bev Lewis. Thank you for supporting Denise and I over the years as we have raised our family and built our business together. Your encouragement and support for us, and your tolerance with me as a son-in-law, means more to me than you will ever know.

To my mentor and predecessor, James Norris, CFP®. I want to thank James and his wife, Jan, for the opportunity to join the firm back in 2004. I was green to the business, so I appreciate them allowing me to come into the business and helping me make a difference in our clients' lives. James helped to not only teach me the business of financial planning and investments, but he also showed me the importance of always doing what is best in the interest of our clients.

TABLE OF CONTENTS

INTRODUCTION

To Do the Right Thing

"Please let everyone know that the coffee is on me today," my father told Wayne, our friend who owned the filling station, feed store, and repair shop near our farm. "It's my birthday, and I think we should celebrate!" He did that almost every year when I was growing up, demonstrating to my brothers and myself his spirit of friendly generosity.

My parents, Max and Jo Ann Miller, ran a diversified livestock and row-crop operation in northwest Missouri, just south of Maryville. My dad was born and raised on our Century Farm near Graham, MO. He also ran a successful property and casualty insurance business and served on the county mutual insurance board for more than thirty years. I am blessed to have been raised by Max Miller, a man of the highest character who modeled it in his three sons in everything he did. A hardworking, friendly, family man—he has always emphasized doing the right thing, reaching out to help others, and treating people right.

As I work in our business today as a financial advisor, helping others find the best path to a prosperous retirement, I think a lot about the life lessons my father taught us. One being the measure of success is the quality of your relationships and what you can do to make a difference in someone's life.

Although I now work in the financial world, I am very proud of my rural roots. I received my degree in Animal Science with a Business minor at Kansas State University, but the first part of my college days were at Northwest Missouri State University, the alma mater of both my mother and father. And it was there that I met a young woman named Denise Lewis who would become my wife— and eventually the vice president of our firm. Later, I'll tell you a story about how I knew she was the one for me.

I am the youngest of three brothers. My oldest brother, Jeff, is a rodeo-stock contractor and rancher in central Nebraska. My other brother, Steve, lives not far from me and represents the third generation of our family to be in the property and casualty insurance business. He and his two sons also manage an extensive cattle operation, Galaxy Beef, LLC, running more than eight hundred head of brood cows in multiple locations throughout Missouri. Our father taught us all to enjoy hard work and to extend a hand of friendship and service to others.

Today, at age eighty-five, our father can see that his generosity took root in us. One of my brothers occasionally even carries on our father's coffee tradition at a cafe in our hometown. I enjoy putting on events for our clients and employees, plus organizing tailgate parties at college football games. It's a small price to pay to bring friends and family together for a great time.

I was a senior in high school when my mother, Jo Ann Miller, died of cancer. That was so long ago, but I know that it was she who developed my creative side. I remember her drawing with me when I was young and teaching me how to wrap Christmas presents. I must say, today I am still better than anyone in the family at this skill!

After earning my degree from KSU and following a yearlong stint as a Purina Mills salesman in Kansas, I returned home to the farm. Dad was then preparing to focus solely on his insurance business and retire from farming. So I came back to Missouri, where my brother Steve and I ran the operation together for a while.

Denise and I were wanting to start a family, and after a few years of farming, I decided to see what I could do with my college education and entered the world of finance. I went out and bought a new suit, put together my resume, and called on some banks and people I knew. Soon I found myself in training to become a loan officer at a bank in Maryville, Missouri. That led to another position at a bank in Savannah, Missouri, which led to another position as vice president of a bank in Red Oak, Iowa. And that's where I live and work today. After five years with that bank, I joined our current financial-services firm in 2004.

Each step has led to the next along my path. All of those experiences have served me well in developing my career. I will always value my days working in agriculture. Here in rural Iowa, in the Midwest, I work today with families that have a wide variety of backgrounds—and many, like mine, have their roots in agriculture. Not only can I talk the talk, but I understand where they are coming from when they tell me of their concerns and dreams—and that helps me to have insight into how to serve them better.

The puzzle

As far back as I can remember, I have enjoyed helping others and working to figure out difficult puzzles. Not being willing to just take things at face value but really trying to understand why and how things work. Those are two main attributes that I believe help make me ideally suited for the field I work in today. I enjoy the challenge of getting to know people and their situations and then helping them assemble the many pieces of a financial plan. A plan that will help them work toward their goals.

Serving others is also fundamental to my foundation as a Christian, a man of faith. I believe one way we serve others is to educate them about their possibilities and opportunities, to help them see a better way. I feel it is our responsibility to help others better themselves. As we do so, we also better ourselves and our families. I am very grateful to be able to make a good living as we help our clients, but I am very mindful that it is not all about the money. Denise and I look around our office at those who work with us and realize that this firm is the source of support for several families. I am both pleased and humbled to have been given this responsibility.

As a firm we work with a diverse group of clients in a region that includes several states. We help them to recognize the "what if" questions in life: "What if the market dropped right before we retired—would we be okay?" or "What if I were to die unexpectedly—would my spouse and family be okay?", "What if my daughter got divorced, How would be the best way to help her?" Those are just a few of the many questions that folks ask. Our goal is to help bring a sense of order into their future financial picture where they may only see potential chaos.

Once we can recognize the questions, it's usually a matter of putting the right tools to work for them. Selecting and aligning the right pieces for their puzzle, if you will. For instance, the goal may not always be to try to earn the highest-possible rate of return for our investment clients. The goal may be to help make sure that our clients' resources do what they want them to do for them for the long term. Our goal is to help address the unknown and to help answer the "what if" questions that everyone faces at some time.

When I meet with our clients or folks considering working with our firm, I try to explain that it's not just about how much money they have but rather how much life they can create with it. What do the resources that they have acquired represent for them? Just what do they want to do with it? What is its purpose?

For some, I learn that it is highly important that they leave a significant legacy. For those clients, we do our best to design a plan to help accomplish their stated goal. Others have told me, more or less, "Throw my last dollar into the casket with me when you shut the lid." In other words, they intend to leave nothing, and if that is their desire, then we don't plan for a legacy. However, many people who would like to leave money to their heirs or a charity, may not see how they could manage to do so. In that case, we talk about the options. We explore options to see how they may be able to do more for others without selling themselves or their families short. We examine their specific "what-ifs."

"I really don't know much about how I should plan or invest," people sometimes tell me. And my reply is often that, "I really don't expect that you would. That's why you have come in to see me." I often explain that it's like going to see a doctor when you are sick, or hurt. You don't try to diagnose yourself. You consult with a professional in that field.

For example, I have a client who is a neurosurgeon. He is a brilliant guy—and yet he comes to me for guidance with his finances. That's why I am here. I would not try to perform brain surgery, and I am sure that he would not expect me to know much about it. He does his thing, and I do mine. He helps save lives; and I help him and his wife with their financial lives.

Although we are on the cutting edge of technology in our practice, our firm has been built on old-fashioned values for the last 53 years. Our symbol of success is still a handshake. The technology we utilize is a tool, useful and vital to our firm, but it alone does not build relationships. You can't form a relationship with a website or an online robo-advisor. It's when we deal with people one-on-one that true bonds and lasting relationships are built.

I often think of my father and of his determination to do the right thing and treat people well. It is a value that I am proud to say has spread through our family. I see his courteous and kind-hearted nature in our own children, twenty-four-year-old Jackson and twenty-two-year-old Andrea. They have grown up to be honest and productive adults, and that is what legacy is all about—values more than money. We should always strive to leave our best to the next generation.

It's easy to see in our society that money amplifies our influence. When we do wrong, it worsens the damage. When we do right, our resources may do a world of good. I have long believed that if you do the right thing, focusing on strong relationships and solid values, the money will follow. Our firm has been built on that premise.

"Will I be able to retire?"

When people come to see me in our office, often the primary question on their minds, whether they express it outright or not, is; "Will I be able to retire?" "Will we have enough?" Ideally, I'd like to hear those questions when they are in their early fifties, or maybe even their late forties. When they're within several years of retirement, the prospect of starting the next chapter of life begins to get very real for a great many people. But there may still be time to make a significant difference.

With retirement-income planning, our goal is to help you identify where you are today, determine where you want to be, and then build the strategy and the means to help get you there. Sometimes, unfortunately, I have to tell people news that they do not want to hear. They may not have sufficient resources to meet the goals that they have set forth. There may need to be compromises made. They may need to continue working for a while. That is why it is essential to start planning early. You do not want any surprises on the brink of retirement. The most important message of this book is this: "Don't wait, take action!" Don't leave the workforce without a retirement-income plan, and don't wait until the day before you leave to make that plan.

At the retirement stage of life, your years of accumulating resources are essentially behind you. It is now time to start putting those resources to use as an income stream that will last for the rest of your life. No longer will you have years stretching out in front of you in which you can recover from substantial market or resource draining setbacks. Understandably, you may now feel more protective of your nest egg. However, you must not become overprotective. You will still need enough growth potential to overcome inflationary pressures, which may take their toll through the years—and many people these days are living decades in retirement. If you stuff your money in a mattress, you are not safeguarding it. You are squandering its potential.

Planners, not brokers

In our practice we have many clients with relatively modest portfolios, and some with millions of dollars. We work with a lot of middle-class families, both rural and urban. Our clients may have made their living in agriculture and industry; or as business owners; teachers and doctors; federal employees—a wide variety of occupations.

As a whole, most of our clients are not multimillionaires. Our office does, indeed, serve some very wealthy families, but for the most part, I am looking to serve hard-working people who have saved $200,000 to $3 million in investable assets. That describes most of our clients. Most will also have their Social Security and perhaps a pension and real estate assets. Many are blue collar and/or white collar working-class couples who each have been earning salaries ranging from $50,000 to $150,000 or more per year. They may not be considered wealthy by Hollywood standards, but they have been making a solid living while still saving for their future.

In our firm, I am a fully registered investment advisor representative and broker. But if you are looking for someone who says he can always provide the highest return and beat your favorite benchmark, we are probably not a good fit to work together. You will not find that sort of advice in this book. I won't know the best strategy, the best investment, for you until I shake your hand and get to know you. It will depend upon your circumstances, needs, and goals. And as the economy changes and your life changes, the best advice for you may change as well.

You will not find our office always at the top of the market, nor at the bottom when it comes to investment returns. We swing for a lot of base hits instead of home runs. We want the good long-term batting average. Our strategy for winning focuses on the entire season, not to always be wowing the crowd along the way. We believe you need the confidence of a comprehensive plan, not just an investment strategy. You don't want to just do well in your financial accounts. You want to do well in life—and that's more about the money you keep than about the money you make.

Our firm was founded in 1963 in Montgomery County, Iowa, by Mildred Parker as an insurance agency. Selling life insurance in Iowa at the time made her a pioneer among women in the profession. Our firm evolved into full financial services under James Norris, who introduced financial planning and securities into the firm as an investment advisor representative in 1994. James, who had an academic and sales background, became my mentor when I joined the firm in 2004 as a financial advisor. I owe a large debt of gratitude to him and to his wife, Jan, for showing me how to succeed by helping others and by always serving the best interest of our clients. In 2013, Denise and I purchased the firm from the Norris family. Denise joined as vice president after a twenty-six-year career with the Natural Resources Conservation Service. Our firm currently has about $105 million in assets under management.

As a CERTIFIED FINANCIAL PLANNER™ professional, a CFP®, I am a fiduciary, someone who is entrusted in good faith with the responsibility of managing another party's assets. As such, I am legally obligated to always put the interests of my clients ahead of my own. Not all people who identify themselves as financial planners are fiduciaries. They are free to simply provide products they deem suitable, regardless of whether they are in the client's best interest or not. My fiduciary obligation is not unlike that of a lawyer or a doctor. I must always work solely on the client's behalf and in his or her best interest, without regard to the effect on my own compensation.

Part of my fiduciary responsibility is to make sure that the client is not facing undue risks. We take a close look at each type of risk and analyze what it could potentially do to their big picture. Those include more than market risk, although that is a consideration. We also consider inflation, taxes, the risk of premature death, and even the risk of prolonged life. In the chapters ahead, we will be looking at each of those in detail. We will be working out the pieces to the puzzle.

It was not a big stretch for me to become a fiduciary when I became a CFP®. It means, basically, doing the right thing—and that is how I intend to live my life. I want to shake your hand, look you in the eye, listen to your stories and dreams, and work alongside you as we solve the retirement puzzle together. If I cannot operate my business in that way, then I am in the wrong profession.

CHAPTER 1

A New Phase of Life

"What are you doing this weekend?" I asked my father one day shortly after he retired.

"I haven't really thought about it," he said. "You know, once you are retired, every day is a Saturday."

For him, I am sure it seemed that way. He had choices, and he had many interests, relationships, and a lot of different things from which to choose from. He could work in his wood shop, travel, or just sit back when he wished. But as we all know, Saturdays tend not to be lazy days. A lot of people find themselves busier than ever in retirement.

"It's not quite what I expected!" are the words I often hear from recent retirees as they describe the new life that they are leading. Sometimes they exclaim it joyfully. Other times I can sense a small amount of stress in their voice. Oftentimes the joy and the stress may come through at the same time. Many retired couples have long dreamed of traveling, but it is a lot of work. And it is great to spend time with the grandkids, but they can sometimes wear you out.

Some imagine this new free time will be spent on leisure activities. Some remain deeply involved in their careers, perhaps as a consultant, or working part time. Others want to stay busy as volunteers. Some play golf. Some try a new hobby or start a new business. Many like to travel, but when that's out of your system, then what?

One thing that we can be certain of is that many more people will be joining the retirement ranks in the very near future. Census information now tells us that it is estimated that approximately ten thousand baby boomers are now retiring every day! The generation that helped build the Social Security system will now be drawing out more and more, as a younger generation with fewer workers contributes less to the system. U.S. Government Accounting Office studies indicate that the system's solvency is at stake without major reforms. If you are in your sixties, you may not see much change. If you are younger, you certainly may see significant change. You can probably count on it. We'll address these potential changes later on.

What I hear from many folks in retirement is that they are now busier than they were when they were working! They may have imagined leisurely hours spent on new hobbies or doing whatever they want, but that is often not the case. Very rarely does anyone just shut down when they retire. The way you live and the way you spend your time and resources during your working years often reflects how you will probably be living and spending your time and resources during your retirement. Very rarely do we see anyone throttle clear down if you have been used to operating at warp speed!

I work with a hard-working couple who run a farming operation and own multiple rental properties, and both spouses have recently received an inheritance as well. During their working years, they lived comfortably, but also somewhat frugally. As a result, they have accumulated several million dollars, and it's hard for them to allow themselves to spend any of it. They are having a hard time adjusting their lifestyle to enjoy the prosperity they now have.

Part of my job is to help such couples come to terms with what they want to do with their resources and what they want their resources to do for their families, and society. Do they want to leave it all to their children? Or grandchildren? Do they want to enjoy some of it themselves? Do they have a desire to leave it to charity? Certainly, they want to be good stewards of their wealth, but they need to realize that it is also okay if they allow themselves to enjoy a portion of it. Often it's just a matter of getting them to recognize that. It may be the fact that they remember what it was like to not have much that drives them to continue to live so frugally. Understanding what their resources can do for the betterment of those around them, can often help to abate the fear and uncertainty they feel.

By contrast, other couples—and this is a story that we see more commonly—are hoping to retire but do not have the adequate resources needed. They may have lived a rather in-the-moment life and did not save much for the future. They may have basically spent it all along the way. In an ideal world, I prefer to try explaining this to folks when they are in their forties or fifties. "Well here is what I see," I may have to tell them, "It appears you have been spending around $150,000 a year, but with the assets you have set aside so far, it appears you are not going to be able to sustain that level of income later in life."

Often they may have become accustomed to a lifestyle that is not sustainable long term. How comfortable will they be going down to a $40,000 a year income in retirement? I can tell you that in my experience, they will probably not be too thrilled about it. They may need to take immediate corrective action now—both on what they are spending and what they are saving. Otherwise they may find themselves in a situation where they may be unable to stop working. Or, if they do, they might find themselves looking for a job in retirement to help sustain their lifestyle.

In these type of situations, what I try to do is approach it from a matter-of-fact point of view. I will never judge someone because they may have not saved as much as they should have along the way. What I often tell folks is "Whatever has happened up till now is in the past. We can't go back and change it. We are here now, so let's try to focus and make a difference in your picture going forward. You have taken the first step by coming in to see me, so let's work together to make a difference going forward."

Excitement and anxiety

The transition into retirement is certainly exciting, but for some, it can feel quite challenging and sometimes troubling. How do you answer people when they ask you what you do? You could respond in dozens of different ways no doubt, but most people identify themselves with their job or career. That is why the loss of a job or ending a career may be very difficult—whether the loss is through layoff or voluntary retirement.

Moving on from your job may be fully your choice, and yet you may still feel that pang inside, a sense of emptiness. For some folks it can almost feel like mourning. Many people in the workforce spend more time with their coworkers than they do with their spouse and kids. Their work may become the source of their circle of friends, and their social life. Unfortunately, it often becomes harder to keep up those connections when you leave the workforce. I actually try to address those feelings with my new clients. I am not a psychologist, but I do know that filling that void has a lot to do with planning a happy and satisfying retirement.

Planning how you will fill your time and who you will spend it with may be as important as making sure you have the adequate resources.

"Now that you will have all of these hours that you will not be at work," I ask, "how will you fill them? Who will you be spending your time with? What are you going to be doing?" When I am talking to a husband and wife, I ask them "Have you talked about that? You will be seeing a lot more of each other—is that going to go well?" This can sometimes bring a smile and a chuckle from each of the spouses, but sometimes you can see a little uncertainty and apprehension as well. I know that it was an adjustment when Denise and I began working together recently at our office! It has gone smoothly for us—and I also want it to go well for others.

Most retirement-age couples may have already experienced the "empty nest." They may recall how happy and sad they were at the same time when their kids went off on their own. Now along comes this other big change in which the spouses may be spending a lot more time together. That may be either joyful, or not. Togetherness can also bring stress, and sometimes even stress on a marriage. Unfortunately, we have seen couples where one or both spouses have begun overeating, or even drinking, to deal with these changes, this new stress. I hope folks won't ever hesitate to seek help if they could potentially see those situations occurring.

In addition to other changes at this time, there is another new life adjustment to deal with. Those regular employment paychecks stop. A major part of what our office does is help our clients to get that income flowing again. Preparing for when the paychecks stop. Our aim is to help you recreate those income streams that you were accustomed to during your working career. That is the goal of retirement- income planning. You have been accustomed to those income rhythms over the years, whether you are an employee, or a self-employed entrepreneur. Now it is time to position your savings so that your income continues as you settle into what hopefully will be a long and happy retirement.

I understand the misgivings. I know that the excitement of retiring almost always comes with a tinge of anxiety and uncertainty. No matter how much money you have, you are bound to wonder what comes next. Will you really be able to do this? Am I sure the time is right? If you are thinking that retirement means the end of all stress, think again. Yes, you are gaining much more freedom, but life goes on, and challenges arise. What you worry about in retirement bears little resemblance to what you may have worried about when you were younger.

It's about time

When you were younger, time was a rather abstract concept. You saw many years stretching out before you, with plenty of opportunities. You figured that you would have time to get around to doing some of those things later. Saving for retirement? Buying life insurance? These may not have been top of mind for you. If you were saving, it was to buy a house, perhaps, or to put your children through college one day.

Then as you began to raise your family, time may have begun to feel a bit more pressing. You felt greater responsibilities, and you marveled at how fast those youthful twenties had passed. Now and then you pictured yourself in retirement someday, and hopefully you resolved to start saving at a faster clip. Whether you realized it or not, time was your ally then. If desired, you could pursue a more aggressive investment strategy, and even if things turned south, you could just wait for the next wave to sweep you forward. Time was on your side!

That awareness of growing older often accelerates into a sense of urgency as the decades sweep past. As I write this, I am fifty-two years old. My wife and I still have a lot to accomplish, but we also recognize that a good part of our working careers are behind us. That makes it all the more important that we clearly identify our goals, financial and otherwise, and organize our life toward reaching them. Some of those aches that we now feel, and the gray hair we are starting to see, are stark reminders that time is marching on and we, like everyone, need to keep moving forward!

It's about time. As the years slip by, it's high time to get going in earnest. The concerns of your past are behind you, for the most part. These are no longer the days when your children are skinning their knees, coming home with their report cards, or even learning to drive. They hopefully have now made their grades, and you are making yours. The things that once seemed to be such a big deal feel less so now, and what had seemed so distant is now at your doorstep.

This is the time of life when your thoughts turn more and more to your priorities. What is most important to you, and what can you still change to emphasize what matters most? How can you make a difference? What do you want to do with the remainder of your years? That could be quite a long time, and those years can be some of your best, if you set out to make them that way. Do you know where you are heading? Do you have a plan to get there?

Hopefully you saved, you have gathered your eggs. You have tucked them away in your nest. All those years, as you set aside something for the future, you were lining that nest for a comfortable retirement. Now, in your sixties or seventies, it is time to see what will hatch. These thoughts are a lot broader than those that occupy the mind of a younger person. The concerns that weigh on you now are far different, and you are now thinking more and more about your life accomplishments and dreams.

Some may involve money and how it's managed—taxes, inflation, interest rates, and maybe the volatility of the market. Those are among some of the perennial issues to address, and with age, they become more imperative. You didn't think about those things very much when you were in your twenties or thirties. Back then, you basically concerned yourself with having enough money to spend for the present, to do the things you wanted to do. Now, you are trying to make sure that you will have enough money to do things now, and in the future. In your fifties and sixties, many also tend to be in their peak earning years. Hopefully you have the money at hand for immediate needs. My goal is to help you be able to continue to meet those needs year after year throughout retirement.

The nature of time, when you are at this stage, has shifted dramatically. It is bound to have an influence on your financial and investment attitude, and style. Many want to take a more protective stance, which calls for a more conservative approach. You may have to switch gears from the come-what-may way that you handled money when you were younger. In a volatile market, your old strategy, or lack of one, could backfire on you. But then time was on your side.

But at this stage the time to recover from these periods of volatility has now grown shorter for you.

Often it calls for a careful balance. This may be a time to reduce your exposure to risk—but ironically, too little risk can be a risk in itself. A trained financial advisor can help you find that balance and the appropriate amount of risk for you and your circumstances. Again, you cannot be 100 percent risk-averse, and an advisor who understands what you are facing, including inflation, will help guide you along your journey. We will be looking more closely at that range of risks in the pages ahead.

I know how you feel. You share a common concern with so many others on the edge of this major change. It's not so much a matter of how much money you have, but whether you have enough to see you through. To do the things you want. To live the retirement you had envisioned. Over the years I have worked with many people at this stage of their life, and I have helped to keep them on track. I have given them the guidance that they need to support themselves long term. This is what I do as a retirement income planner.

CHAPTER 2

In Pursuit of Dreams

You would never know that my wife, Denise, has multiple sclerosis. The disease is mostly under control, and we are fortunate as she has experienced few problems over the years. And yet we both know that MS is a progressive disease. We concede that we do not know what the future will hold for her and our life together.

Life is all about priorities. At every turn, each of us should choose what matters most, and choose wisely. Your personal circumstances, the things that nobody may understand except those closest to you, have much to do with whether you skew toward living only for today, or saving for tomorrow. Priorities and dreams are different for everyone.

I am a believer in balance. I feel that we must enjoy life as we go, for we all know tomorrow may never come. However, we must not live *all* in the moment. It is one thing to be carefree, but quite another to be careless. Especially with your resources. I believe it is never responsible to squander money without thought of the consequences, nor is it responsible to hoard money without thought to the consequences.

Living responsibly means making your best choices day by day about what matters most, even when that means postponing immediate gratification. As life and circumstances change, the best choices may differ day to day. These may change from holding hands on the back porch and enjoying the sunset, to planning an elaborate trip, to adding another thousand dollars to the grandchildren's college account.

Denise and I recognize that life is short, so we try to make each day count. We aim to do the right thing and treat people the right way. Knowing what might happen with her health, we have planned for the contingencies and prepared for financial needs that could present themselves. Blessed today with able bodies, we will continue to work hard and stay on course toward an abundant future. Still, we understand the uncertainties, and we try to enjoy life now, traveling and enjoying time with our families when we can.

Sometimes when I meet with new clients, often they will reminisce about their parents' lives. "You know, it's great that Mom and Dad left us all this inheritance," they may say, "but they never really enjoyed any of it themselves. I just wish they had taken the time to stop worrying and start living." The prevailing sentiment is that they would much rather have spent more time with Mom and Dad enjoying the fruits of their labors, rather than have gotten more money left to them when they were gone.

It's true that you may get into trouble if you indulge in champagne tastes on a beer budget—but if you have the wherewithal for a champagne toast to your golden years, I feel that you owe yourself that small indulgence. I once heard someone say "Why make the journey if you are not going to enjoy the trip a little along the way?" I wish I remembered who had said that quote. I think we all owe it to ourselves to take some of that message to heart.

Identifying priorities

Life happens, and sometimes people get off course through no fault of their own. And yet, often we can anticipate and plan for such contingencies. You can expect the unexpected. You might not be able to prevent every disruption, but you need not let the unexpected ruin your retirement and your life. Often there are tools that may allow us to help you mitigate these risks.

As you approach retirement and your final days on the job, or running your business, you naturally will think more and more about what you may have always wanted to do and accomplish. How will you be remembered after you have left this earth? Sometimes, couples have never really talked about these things. It is certainly a good idea to do so before launching into retirement.

In other words, you must identify your priorities and decide how you will go about attaining them. You might even want to put them in writing as a tangible part of your retirement plan. One of the things we encourage our clients, and future clients, to do is to actually write down the things they want to do in the first five years of retirement, ten years, and so on. We feel this actually helps them to visualize what the next few years could look like and how to plan for them.

Establishing a timeline for meeting your objectives may help you bring order to your planning, to your priorities.

It has been said that retirees often have their "go-go years," their "go-slow years," and their "no-go years." New retirees typically start focusing on all those things that they have been putting off through the years. They may still feel an abundance of energy and a desire to venture out to see the world. These are the go-go years. When I work with couples on their retirement-income planning, we talk about that and try to prepare for it. We often can anticipate that the curve of their spending during retirement will not be linear. They usually spend more on discretionary expenses in the first decade or so, and then that will taper off as they get well into their seventies and into their eighties. They will then be entering the years when they may be going slower. Instead of that trip to Paris, they will be more content to attend their grandchildren's ballgames in their hometown. They may be going to the doctor's office more often than their favorite restaurants.

For some, the next step is the no-go years. This is usually late in life, at a time when spending may actually increase again—although this time not for discretionary expenses but for such costs as long-term care or home care. Often, that is the typical financial curve during retirement: a burst of spending, and then a leveling off until old age. "When I quit traveling, or my volunteer activities," people tell us, "my spending will go down," and that may well be true to an extent. However, what we typically have seen is that because of increased medical and healthcare costs, the spending does not necessarily decrease as much as you might think it would in this phase. We help plan for that. Although we understand that retirement spending is cyclical, we want you to have enough resources to support yourself in those later years.

How healthy are you? How long do people typically live in your family? The answers to those questions must also be figured into the equation. Once again, a sensible retirement-income plan needs to take into consideration your unique circumstances. What is right for someone else might be absolutely wrong for you. By working with a professional, you can design a plan that is suitable for you and your particular situation.

Plotting your course

Through my experience, I have found that people who were spenders during their working years may have trouble changing those habits during their retirement years. Likewise, those who for years have been inclined to be savers will continue that trend. Leopards don't often change their spots entirely.

Therefore, we often project spending on most living expenses for recent retirees to be 80–100 percent of what it was before retirement. Especially in the beginning. In most instances, we don't see that falling off right away. Sure, some expenses might ease back—the cost of commuting to work, for example—but new ones may arise, such as the cost of driving to see the grandkids, going to car shows, or to take golf lessons. During your working years, you may have tended to spend more on weekends. In retirement, when every day is like a Saturday, you can imagine how the expenses could potentially add up.

Whether you are a saver or a spender by nature, your goals and your dreams need to be aligned with your resources. Whether you can do more than you think you can—or less—either way you need to know about it as soon as possible so that you can make the necessary adjustments. That's the overarching purpose of retirement-income planning. Our goal as a retirement income planning firm is to help set you on a course of reasonable expectations.

As I work with new clients to set up their plan, we start with a snapshot, or inventory, of where they are today. These plans include all of their current resources and income streams. Then we look down the road to their destination. How do we get from point A to point B? I ask them about where they want to go, and then together, we look at whether they have the resources to get there. If they fall short, we may need to look at whether we can make any adjustments to their current picture or plans.

That may make it possible to reach the objective. Unfortunately, sometimes we have to adjust the objective itself. In other words, occasionally they may say, "I would like to have $100,000 a year, inflating at 3 percent for income when I retire," and they just don't have enough assets in place, or a method to accumulate them, to get to that point. We may have to adjust the target as well.

Toward that end, I will also work with clients on their budgeting, if that is necessary and desired as a part of their planning. Some people balk at the word budget, but they need to understand that following a spending plan is what all people, wealthy or not, often must do to get a grip on their finances. Can you imagine any company or organization operating without a budget? It is a fundamental responsibility, whether at the individual, corporate, or governmental level. It shows good stewardship and fiscal responsibility.

A budget can be as complex or as simple as you want it to be. It can just be a measure of inflows and outflows, or you can track and list details via an online budgeting program. Whatever the method, it comes down to this: the money going out should not outpace the money coming in. In working with clients, I know that a clear budget is an indispensable step toward making sure that retirement goals are realistic and attainable.

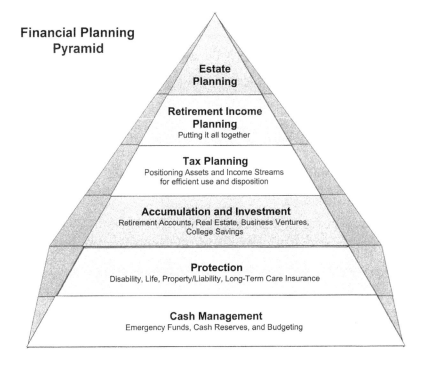

Financial Planning Pyramid

Estate Planning

Retirement Income Planning
Putting it all together

Tax Planning
Positioning Assets and Income Streams
for efficient use and disposition

Accumulation and Investment
Retirement Accounts, Real Estate, Business Ventures,
College Savings

Protection
Disability, Life, Property/Liability, Long-Term Care Insurance

Cash Management
Emergency Funds, Cash Reserves, and Budgeting

Everything in good order

As you identify the priorities for your life in retirement, you will need to keep certain documents available that will help you define your direction. In order for us to help our clients, they need to share these with us. They are essential in devising a financial plan.

The list of documents needed are diverse and slightly different for each person depending upon the complexity of their financial situation and the objective of the planning. But when it comes to planning for retirement income, there is a basic core of documentation needed in most cases.

We will need to see your tax returns, of course, and usually for more than one year. By looking at a series of tax returns, I will be able to recognize trends that we may need to address. From year to year, the flow of income and expenses should become obvious. I will also be able to see the type of tax-qualified contributions you are making, the kind of deductible expenses you have, your philanthropic inclinations, and much more.

In addition to the tax returns, I also need to see copies of all your current statements: investment statements, IRAs, nonqualified-investment accounts, and others. I will also need records of your current and future income streams, such as Social Security statements and pension-benefit statements. What I try to put together is a profile of where you are today and where you are headed. I will also want to see documentation and statements for any life insurance, disability, long-term care, and other policies that you may have. These are utilized to assess your current levels of risk protection in place. Protection against this type of "what-ifs" in life may be critical to constructing a plan that will help protect against short-term events that can have long term consequences regarding ones retirement income.

I will also be looking to see whether you have established an emergency fund. Our experience has shown us that it is hard to make a long-range plan if a short-term event will trip it up. If you do not have emergency savings, where will you get the money if your car breaks down, or your furnace fails, or if any number of unexpected expenses come your way? If your only recourse is to borrow money from your 401(k), or to liquidate a ROTH IRA, you may be compromising your future. That is why I am a big believer in building up a short-term emergency fund and then fully funding your retirement accounts. The emergency fund may help prevent you from impeding the progress of your other retirement accounts.

Despite the importance of retirement planning, many people do not get around to it. Some people tell themselves that they do not have sufficient resources to warrant doing any financial planning. That is simply not true. No matter what stage of life you are in, or where you are financially, you need to plan. How can you possibly know where you are going with any sense of confidence unless you have reliable GPS, or at least a good map? Your financial plan is your road map to the destination that you have chosen. Without it, you may not get to choose your destination. You may end up somewhere you didn't want to go.

"I'll worry about it later," people sometimes tell me—but "later" by definition means you will be giving yourself less time to make a difference. Ideally, I would like to start meeting with folks when they are still in their thirties or forties because of the time they have to still make a long-term difference. If you wait until you are sixty, yes, you still can make a difference, but not nearly as much as you might have been able to make if you had started a decade or so earlier.

"Well, I just don't have that much money anyway," is another reason I sometimes hear folks say regarding their unwillingness to plan. I sometimes have to remind prospective clients that they are going to retire one way or the other—either standing up or lying down. If their plan is to work until they fall over, then they will be retiring for good. But if they still want to enjoy retirement, they need a plan.

It's usually not a matter of the amount of wealth; it's a matter of planning for what comes next, and then making the most of what resources you have and where you are.

These subjects are sometimes hard to talk about, and I understand that. Perhaps there are family issues that they would rather not discuss. Sometimes people are embarrassed regarding their current situation. They feel that they have not done as good a job as they should have, and now they hesitate to ask for help or to share that with anyone. That's unfortunate, but I know that is what sometimes lies behind a reluctance to take action. Sometimes people recognize that they should have been saving over the years rather than spending so freely, and so they try to put off the time of reckoning. And by delaying the inevitable, they thereby may make their situation worse.

I sometimes have to have very frank discussions with people about their spending habits and other financial decisions. But, I would hope that they would expect that from me. And I would hope that they would listen to me in the way they would listen to a doctor giving them medical advice. Ignoring medical advice can put your physical health in danger. Ignoring advice from an experienced CFP® such as myself could possibly put your fiscal health in danger as well. We need to be forthright with each other, disclosing all pertinent information and committing to an ongoing course of action, not unlike that of a treatment plan from your doctor. I can help point you in the right direction, but I cannot make it work for you. As with medical treatment, much of your success in financial planning will be based upon your willingness to follow the suggestions given.

I am not here to judge. I am here to help, if at all possible. Those who come in to our office are seeking assistance in one way or another. Let me emphasize again: the sooner you get started, usually the better off you will be. You cannot be sure what life will send your way. Many retirees have had to downgrade their lifestyle due to unexpected expenses or circumstances. Sometimes something has to give, whether it is your spending or your expectations. Others have been able to upgrade their lifestyle due to an unexpected inheritance or some other windfall. Whatever your situation, you can be sure that you are not alone. I have seen a wide array of scenarios in my career, and I vow to stand by my clients to weather whatever storms life may throw at them.

The task before us is one of organizing and preparing for your journey. Beginning with the end in mind, we will examine your goals and priorities and then construct your plan. Once we identify your destination, we will help chart the course to get you there.

CHAPTER 3

Who Needs a Plan Anyway?

"What I do is so different that I don't think anyone can help me," is something I heard one time from a new client who had a very unique occupation. He was a self-employed jeweler that custom built high-end jewelry and sold the pieces to upscale jewelry stores for resale. His biggest concern was, "What if I were to become disabled? What if I lost my eyesight or dexterity in my fingers? What if I could no longer practice my craft?"

He wasn't particularly worried about retirement or outliving his money. He wasn't really concerned with anything regarding retirement planning because as long as he could work and make a great living, he could put some money away. In his particular situation, his "what if" was also not about what happened if he died prematurely. He had purchased life insurance. He was worried about living. Living with a disability that is.

He was concerned about how he would be able to feed his family and provide for them and how he would be able to put anything away for their future if he could no longer be a jeweler. Everyone's situation is unique, and every situation requires planning that is specific to their situation. There is no cookie-cutter plan that fits everyone.

In his case, we worked to address the activities that not only allowed him and his wife to better sleep at night, but were also the items that could potentially prevent their retirement income plan from ever having a chance to get off the ground. His unique planning, based primarily on protection planning initially, was the first step in a long-term income planning strategy. While he was still working, we were able to secure disability protection for him to at least assure that his family would have some immediate resources to fall back on in case of a disabling injury that prevented him from working as a jeweler.

Next, we looked at their emergency funds. If he did become disabled or couldn't work, were there resources readily available to get them through for some period of time until the disability policy kicked in? Or in case a major expense came along in the meantime? Without these first two strategies in place, the rest of their needed retirement income plan could be put in jeopardy.

After building up their emergency funds, we looked at his current level of contributions to his retirement accounts. We were able to show him and his wife that by making just a few adjustments to their spending habits, they should be able to both substantially increase their retirement plan contributions as long as they were both working. Also, we were able to better position his existing portfolio into a multi-bucket system for income planning. We positioned a portion of what he already had accumulated so that it would generate a known income stream for them in the future at retirement. This also helped both spouses be confident that they at least wouldn't be penniless in retirement. We will take a closer look at these types of strategies in Chapter 9.

So were we able to completely solve his/their concerns? No, there were trade-offs that had to be made. It was not a perfect solution. There are still risks that they face. But at least he and his wife are both now more confident knowing that they have a plan and some protection in place in case the worst case happens.

This is what planning is all about. It is not a perfect process. It never is. It is working to best control the things that you can, and working to control the effects or damage from the things you cannot. And this process is different for everyone.

Serving a niche

So who needs a plan? In our practice, we work with a vast array of clients and professions. In our part of the country we have clients involved in all different types of professions and careers. Even though we are in a rural area, we serve a very diverse array of clients. Ours is not an area such as you might see in Silicon Valley where maybe 80 percent of an advisors clients are going to be involved in one industry, or from one major employer.

We also are not a practice that limits our clientele only to one particular profession, group, or specialty. These firms can be very successful in the right setting and in the right areas. But this is not how we have chosen to structure our practice. We regard ourselves as highly trained general practitioners with a very specific set of skills. The skills needed to provide our clients with *Retirement Built to Last*.

But with this being said, we do have a few specific niches, or groups of clients, that we work with throughout the country. The members of each of these groups usually share some common concerns, obstacles, and objectives. These groups usually also share a unique set of retirement benefits, which we utilize to design their plans around.

Federal Employees

One particular group that we work with throughout the country are federal employees. As I mentioned earlier in the book, my wife Denise is a former federal employee, having worked twenty-seven years for the Natural Resources Conservation Service, a division of the United States Department of Agriculture, prior to joining our firm. What prompted me to take an interest in really diving in and learning the specifics of the federal benefits system and the challenges faced by these employees; all links back to one specific incident.

Besides having a vested interest in Denise's benefits because of her being my spouse, it came to my attention that the majority of federal employees were not really receiving the guidance they needed regarding their benefits. Denise came home one day and said that her human resources person told all of the employees at a meeting that day that they did not need to list beneficiaries on their Thrift Savings retirement accounts. This person said it was not needed because the funds would all go to their estates anyway, and therefore, their family would end up getting the money. Yikes!

This was the "advice" they were receiving? True, if no beneficiaries are listed, the funds will eventually end up with your heirs—or at least what is left of the funds! This person forgot to mention that by doing it this way, these proceeds may now be subject to the delays and expense of the probate process. They also forgot to mention that instead of being able to receive the benefits in maybe a week or so as a result of a beneficiary designation, they may have to wait up to nine months or more until the estate has been settled. Also, if this participant doesn't have a will or a trust in place, the funds may not end up in the hands of whom they would have wanted after it goes through the probate courts. So needless to say, I immediately urged Denise to go ahead and fill out her beneficiary designations properly!

From that point, in 2008, I made it my mission to find a way to fully learn and understand the federal retirement and employee benefits systems. I attended two separate specialized-training classes on federal benefits to become fully educated on this somewhat complicated set of benefits. I had come to realize after talking to Denise and several other federal employees that there was a real disconnect between these employees and the guidance they were receiving regarding their benefits.

Since 2008, I have provided federal benefits seminars for many different employee groups throughout the Midwest. These groups have included the FAA, the TSA, the USDA, the Federal Court System, the Dept. of Reclamation, the ATF, and the National Parks Service. With Denise now having joined our firm, along with Associate Advisor and Investment Adviser Representative Andrew Focht, who also had formerly been a federal employee, we intend to continue to make working with this group a focus of our practice moving forward.

Protecting our rural legacy

Our firm, located approximately an hour from Omaha, NE, two hours from Des Moines, IA, and three hours from Kansas City, MO, is located amongst some of the most fertile and productive farmland in the Midwest. Because of our location between these three metro areas, we have clients from all walks of life and different parts of the country. But one thing that many people in this part of the country have in common is that somewhere in their family lineage, they more than likely may have a tie somewhere back to the land and the rural way of life. It may be their great-great grandfather on their mother's side, or even farther back in their linage, but somewhere there is often a tie back to the rural way of life.

Because of this tie to agriculture, most people in the Midwest have a great respect for the land and the legacy that it holds. So as a firm, this respect for the land and the desire to keep that legacy in the family is something that we take very seriously. This is especially true for those families who still directly work the land and make their livelihood in agriculture. Therefore, working with rural families on succession and financial estate planning has become another area of focus in our business.

Having been raised on a working livestock and crop farm and ranch in northwest Missouri, and having made my living working that operation before joining the financial world, I understand the needs of rural families and the issues they face. But now, I am that off-farm heir that is not involved in the daily operation of our farm and ranch. I still care, and I am connected to the operation—but in a different way. It will always be part of my heritage, but it is just not my everyday way of life anymore. Because of this connection, it affords me the insight into what is important for rural families as they work to protect their legacy.

In farm families today, it is not uncommon for there to be one or two children who stay to work the operation while other siblings leave to pursue other careers. And there is nothing wrong with that.

With the mobility and opportunities afforded to young people in rural areas today, it truly is sometimes hard to have an answer to the question, "How are you going to keep 'em down-on-the-farm?" Because of these situations where some heirs are directly involved in working the farm or ranch and others are not, it can make succession and financial estate planning very challenging for some rural families.

This is where we can help. We work with rural families to help address the tough questions. Questions such as when it comes to dividing up the estate amongst the kids. Is "equal" really "fair" to all parties involved? If not, what type of tools or strategies are available to help address this?

For example, if one sibling stayed on the farm to work beside his parents to help build up their operation, is "equal" really "fair" when it comes time to divide everything up? The siblings that went off and did their own thing—do they deserve as big a share as the sibling who helped increase the estate of their parents to its current size? Mom and Dad may want to be "fair," but they also recognize the work the on-farm child put into the operation. They wouldn't have what they do today without the work that the farming heir put into the operation.

So how do you handle this? What is the best avenue to take? There is no cookie-cutter answer for this. Each family must decide for themselves. But oftentimes, the parents may look for ways to help reward the farm heir, or in a sense, pay them for their "sweat equity" above and beyond the value their siblings will receive from the estate. We work to find methods to help them accomplish this.

Or, maybe they want to make sure and keep the land together so the farming heir will always be able to utilize it. The parents may have spent their life building up their legacy, and they want the land to all stay in one unit, in the family name, and not ever be divided. They realize this division could possibly happen if it ended up with the nonfarm heirs or their spouses. So, now they need a strategy or plan to help keep the farmland together while finding a way to equalize the estate assets in a manner that is fair to all parties.

The problem is that in most farm-family estates, the majority of the value of the estate is tied up in the farmland. Based on the elevated farmland values that we see throughout the country today, for some families the land may make up to 70 to 80 percent of the total estate value. So if the goal is to keep the land all together in one farming unit for one heir, where do you find the resources to "equalize" the estate amongst the other heirs? Where is this value going to come from? This again is where we work with clients to address these types of obstacles. These strategies may utilize tools such as life insurance combined with buy/sell agreements or multiple trust agreements. Everyone's situation is unique. We believe everyone deserves a unique solution and strategy designed to protect their own legacy.

Just starting out

As of this writing, our son Jackson is twenty-four, and our daughter Andrea is twenty-two. We are fortunate as they both are working on a plan for starting their adult lives. Jackson is working on a second degree in computer engineering/ management information systems at Iowa State University and has secured a technology based internship with a major manufacturing firm. Andrea is finishing up her under-graduate degree from the University of Northern Iowa this spring in preparation for having recently been accepted into the Doctorate program in Occupational Therapy at Creighton University.

But as I talk with them and others around their age, I realize how it appears that our society has sometimes left many young people woefully unprepared when it comes to managing their financial lives when they are just starting out. For many young people, this period is one of the most exciting and scary times in their lives. Many are starting new jobs, they may be getting married, starting to pay back student loans, buying and licensing their own cars for the first time, renting apartments, starting families, filing taxes for the first time, securing their own health insurance; etc. This list of "first-time" financial events goes on and on! But unfortunately, no one may have given them much guidance about each of these new "firsts" up to this point.

This is where we come in. In our firm we are fortunate to have two Associate Advisors that are both under the age of 35, Andrew Focht, who I mentioned previously and Kaleb Robuck. This helps us to have a unique perspective regarding the challenges facing those that are just starting out on their financial journey. As a firm we believe that it is very important to help the next generations, Gen X, Gen Y, and all Millennials, to learn how to be good fiscal citizens.

Unfortunately, many folks in our industry do not look at this group as worthy of their time or resources as they may not yet have many assets to manage, and the opportunities to profit from assisting them are minimal. This may be somewhat true, but we don't look at it this way. We feel that helping financially educate this group, and assisting them along their fiscal journey, is at the core of our responsibilities as financial advisors. By utilizing the tools and technology afforded to us we can help prepare this generation to be good stewards of their resources and those assets that they will accumulate, or inherit, in the future. Part of Associate Advisor Kaleb Robucks' emphasis in our firm is working with young professionals and families throughout the country. Utilizing the technology platforms available to us today, this allow Kaleb, Andrew, and myself to work with our clients nationwide utilizing many different communication mediums.

We often work with the children of our clients to help prepare them for what lies ahead for them financially. With the permission of their parents, we can help them prepare for the "firsts" that may be soon coming their way. This generation is getting ready to inherit one of the largest amounts of wealth ever seen in history from their baby-boomer parents. The choices they make with this new found wealth may play a dramatic part in the future of our country.

We also work with many young married couples as they prepare to start a family, save for their kids' college education, or buy their first home. We often help guide these folks as they enter the workforce regarding their investment and employee benefit decisions they are going to need to make. As stated before, we often utilize online platforms, asset aggregation tools, and social media tools to collaborate with this generation from a distance as needed.

Changes and opportunities

Someone once said. "The only constant thing in life is change." And as we all know, this is often more true than we realize. Therefore, one of the biggest emphasis in our practice is assisting those who are experiencing change. These changes can be as of a result of a multitude of factors. Things such as retirement, a new grandchild, divorce, starting a new business, death of a spouse, new job, relocation due to new career, recently married, the list goes on and on.

So I'm not sure if this qualifies as a specific niche. But those experiencing these type of changes often need guidance to help them navigate the obstacles and opportunities that come with these changes. Each circumstance is unique and each person going through it is also unique as well. Therefore, unbiased, professional guidance from an experienced professional can often be very valuable during these periods of change.

For example, someone who may have unfortunately just lost their spouse. They may now be facing decisions and launching into a new way of life that is very foreign to anything they have ever experienced before. And unfortunately they often have to make some decisions at a time when they are not truly emotionally stable or even really thinking straight. During this time they also may be receiving advice from well-meaning family members and friends, but this can sometimes just add to the confusion they may be feeling. Therefore, we feel that part of our responsibility during these times is to serve as a pillar of reason and insight. Someone who can provide advice, direction, and stability from an un-emotional standpoint.

It is not that we don't care, or are not very concerned regarding what our client is now going through. We care very deeply about our clients and their families. Many of our clients often become very close friends with me and our staff. So it is very difficult to ever see anyone go through these type of situations. But, we know that part of our responsibilities as fiduciaries is to do what is in the best interest of our clients. And that often includes helping these clients not to make knee-jerk, emotional decisions that could perhaps jeopardize their long term picture. That also is at the core of our responsibility of being a true professional.

Everyone's different

So who needs a plan? We believe everyone does. People from all walks of life have unique challenges and obstacles when it comes to retirement and estate planning. We believe you owe it to yourself to work with someone who will listen to you and take the time to learn about your specific situation. Maybe you do have a very unique situation, like the jeweler mentioned earlier. But there is no way I, or any other planner, will know how to assist you unless you take that first step and talk to someone.

CHAPTER 4

The Future Is in Your Hands

I have some urgent advice for retirees: If you are looking for a place to rest, be careful where you sit, or you could be in for quite a surprise. Take a closer look at that old three-legged stool—the one that you long trusted would be there for you when you needed a rest . . . like when it is time to retire. Time has taken its toll on that stool you'd always counted on. One of the legs is wobbly. One is almost falling off. If you try to use that stool, you might find yourself sprawling on the floor!

Each of those legs represents a source of income that previous generations of retirees have counted upon to secure their financial future. Together they once offered a sturdy and reliable foundation. If you depend solely upon that stool today, however, you could end up in an undignified position. The wobbly leg represents Social Security benefits. The leg that is falling off represents company pensions. That means that many people who are planning for retirement must depend heavily on the third leg—their own savings and investments—to support them. They no longer have a stool. It's more like a pogo stick, and it keeps them hopping.

In this chapter, we will take a look at the changing nature of financial and retirement-income planning for the multitude of baby boomers who are coming of retirement age. Their parents and grandparents entered retirement with at least some sense of confidence that the company and the government would be taking care of them. Today that responsibility has shifted significantly to the individual. Now, for many, it is the resources that they have put away during their working years that will play the major role in seeing them through.

For better or for worse, your future is in your own hands now more than ever. In effect, you may need to create your own pension during your working years, contributing primarily your own resources. That represents a significant challenge and a significant opportunity. Whether or not you rise to the occasion will have a lot to do with the skills and experience of whoever manages your resources—whether that is you, or someone you appoint to the task.

Social Security insecurity

"Well, I've got my Social Security . . ." I have often heard people say. The problem is that some future retirees really don't seem to be thinking about it as a supplement to their retirement income. It's a misconception that reflects the somewhat wishful thinking that maybe it will be enough to see them through their retirement years. For most, unfortunately it will not.

Your Social Security benefit was never intended to fully fund your retirement. The money you may have paid into the system all those years was only meant as a safety net to supplement your other retirement income sources. The system was not set up to pay your way through retirement or to be your caretaker, freeing you of responsibility. In addition, with the changes looming on the horizon, it may become somewhat of an even less dependable source for retirement income depending upon your situation.

People are living longer today than the founders of the Social Security system in the 1930s probably ever imagined. Life expectancy has increased dramatically since the Great Depression era when the system was constructed. Centenarians, those who are 100 years of age or older, were once a rarity. Now they are much more common and medical advances hold out the prospect that people will continue to live increasingly longer.

The baby-boomer generation sometimes is described inelegantly, but quite accurately, as what it looks like when a pig gets eaten whole by a python. We have seen that "Pig-in-a-python" lump moving right along from head to tail through the years. After World War II, the hospital nursery wards overflowed. Growing families demanded resources, and consumer spending followed suit as those children grew to flood the classrooms and went off to college. Behind them, the python contracted as the swell moved on. Today, the baby boomers are beginning to retire, and the pace will continue. The baby boomers are now in the collection stage, with fewer workers in their wake to pay into the system, and this new crop of retirees has every expectation of living for decades longer.

"Pig-in-a-Python" Example

With a huge number of Baby Boomers in the work force, surplus is built up in the Social Security System Reserves.

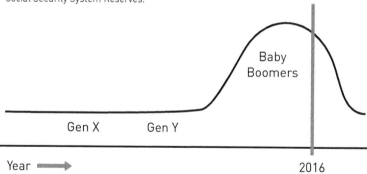

A smaller workforce is paying into the Social Security System. Reserves are being depleted becuause Baby Boomers are living longer than systems anticipated, huge numbers are drawing benefits, and a smaller workforce is paying into the system.

The implications are clear enough, and that is why the Social Security system is in peril and why we hear those perennial proposals on how it should be fixed. Politicians have made adjustments in the past—some benefits have been subjected to taxation, for example—but those changes have only postponed dealing with the fundamental issue, which is fewer workers supporting far more retirees who will collect benefits longer than ever before.

"Will my Social Security payments be there for me?" folks often ask me, and I wholeheartedly believe that the answer is yes. Will the system look different than it does now? Yes, I believe that as well. The baby boomers built up a large reserve with their contributions, but as they move into retirement, that reserve is dwindling. Nonetheless, if you are age sixty or older today (2016), I believe you can expect to receive all, or the vast majority, of your benefits. Even without changes, according to a 2011 study, the Government Accounting Office expects to be able to pay full benefits until 2033, according to the latest projection. After that, the projections show the system would be able to pay out only about 75 percent of the benefits due—that is, unless Congress acts to significantly shore up the system.

The big question is what those changes might be. One proposal has been to raise the normal retirement age. This would not be the first time that Congress has taken that action. It used to be age sixty-five, and now it is either sixty-six or sixty-seven, or a number in between, depending upon your date of birth. It is possible that we could see that rise to perhaps age seventy, or older, for future retirees!

Congress in the past has also raised the threshold level for how much you can earn in income before your Social Security benefit is subjected to tax. This is another method to increase fiscal income. Until 1984, no benefits were taxed. Currently, (2016) if a couple filing a joint return earns more than $32,000, half the benefits could be taxed. If the couple's income exceeds $44,000, up to 85 percent of the benefits could be taxed.

Other suggestions for amending the system have been to use a different means of figuring and applying the cost-of-living adjustment (COLA) each year. Some have called for privatizing some of the investments, meaning the system would put a portion of its securities into the open market. That proposal has not gained much traction, and I don't foresee it happening anytime soon.

One of the popular proposals is to raise the Social Security earnings that are subject to tax. For 2016, only the first $118,500 of a worker's earnings is subject to Social Security tax. Some have suggested raising that significantly in the years ahead or even taxing all earnings with no limit.

From time to time, we also hear proposals for means testing to distribute Social Security benefits. Benefits would be either increased or restricted based upon your current level of earnings and assets, regardless of what you may have or have not paid into the system. Whether it ever comes about is pretty much a matter of the political winds, and it is bound to be a hot button. I believe that means testing punishes the wealthy for doing well. Not only would the higher earners be subjected to tax on a greater proportion of their income, but their benefit also would be restricted because of that higher income. The affluent would be contributing proportionately more and getting back proportionately less.

What do I believe will be the solution? I think Congress will choose a combination of approaches. One way or another, I believe that the system will be sustained. Too many people have too big a stake in it for the government not to take steps to address the projected deficiencies. Even if no reforms are made, it will be fifteen or twenty years before the system needs to cut back on benefits. If action is taken soon, we should be able to expect full benefits to persist considerably longer than that.

So, if you are now on the brink of retirement, take heart. People who are now retirement age as of this writing should be able to figure that they will receive their current projected benefits. When I am working with people in their fifties, I certainly do not take the benefit out of the equation, but I will see if the client wishes to discount it. A fifty-year-old who has been in the workforce for twenty or thirty years may have paid a lot into the system. He or she certainly is going to get something back. The question is, "how much?" We subscribe to a service that helps us to do Social Security analysis for our clients. We use the software to project the effect that something less than the full benefit would have on the course of a retirement. A married couple between the ages of sixty-two and seventy can apply for benefits in a multitude of ways. With so many choices, you can see why professional guidance is a good idea.

Timing it right

I sometimes hear: "I've worked hard my whole life, and now I am sixty-two, and by golly I am not going to wait to take it!" I understand why folks feel that way, but this may not always be the best course of action. One major consideration right at the start is whether you intend to continue working past age sixty-two. If you are under the full retirement age of sixty-six to sixty-seven and you earn more than $15,720 in 2016, you will be giving up a dollar of your benefit for every two dollars you make over that amount. In the year you reach full retirement age, you may earn up to $41,880 before your benefits are reduced. Once you have reached your full retirement age, you can then earn as much as you want without a decrease in your benefit.

Another consideration is your family's tendency toward longevity. How long did your parents live? And just how healthy are you now? If you are in poor health and your father died when he was sixty-eight, then yes, maybe you had better consider taking your benefit now while you still can.

If you do so, however, be very aware of what you are giving up. Your benefit will be 25 percent smaller at age sixty-two than at full retirement age. For every year after age sixty-two, all the way up to age seventy, the benefit will increase 6 to 8 percent, depending upon the year. Those are guaranteed increases in the benefit, and that is in addition to any possible cost-of-living adjustments that may be granted. Once you reach age seventy, there is absolutely no reason to wait to claim your benefit because it does not increase beyond that point except for potential COLAs.

When filing for Social Security benefits, it is not as easy as just saying, "Hey I am ready. Send it to me." This is especially true for married couples, who, though they still have many options for electing benefits, now have fewer options for claiming benefits due to new regulations passed in November 2015. The familiar "file and suspend" rule that we used with clients is discontinued as of May 2016, as well as a change to the "deeming" rules, a strategy also known as "file and file again."

You no longer can file for your benefit and then suspend it so your spouse can begin receiving a spousal benefit while you continue to work, allowing your own benefit to grow each year. Also, when you do file, your benefit now will be the larger of either your own benefit, or the spousal benefit, regardless of your intention. You are now "deemed" to be applying for the maximum benefit for which you are eligible at that time. This eliminated the ability for higher-earning spouses to receive a 50 percent benefit on the lower-earning spouse while allowing their own benefit to grow to age seventy.

The timing of when to turn on benefits is one of many decisions when putting together all of the pieces of the retirement-income plan. Another key factor to remember with Social Security planning is that when one spouse passes away, only one benefit, the larger of the two, will remain for the surviving spouse. It may be important to your plan to allow the larger benefit to grow in case of the early loss of a spouse. This must be considered when looking at implementing a plan for taking Social Security benefits.

Farewell to pensions

Once the bedrock of retirement-income planning, the defined-benefit pension plan unfortunately for many is passing into the history books. Although there are still many retirees who can count on the regular income from a pension sponsored by the company where they worked, or by public entities and the states, most people entering retirement today do not have that benefit. Their companies have long since discontinued their defined-benefit pension programs. We have also seen the difficulties that public pension programs have been facing. Over the years, the responsibility for providing a retirement income has shifted from the employer to the employee.

Since the late 1970s, companies have been moving away from those defined-benefit pension plans in favor of defined-contribution plans—aka the 401(k)s and similar tax-qualified investment programs. Today they are the primary source of retirement income for a great many people.

Why did pensions go by the wayside? A pension is based upon a formula, and as parts of that formula change, the equation may cease to work properly. For one, people today are living a lot longer than they did when many of those pension plans were put into place. Also, interest rates over the last twenty-plus years have been depressed compared to historical norms. As a result of those forces, pension funds found themselves paying out benefits far longer than had ever been expected, and at the same time, interest rates did not sustain the growth of those funds at the level that the actuaries had predicted. Trouble clearly was brewing. The math no longer worked.

The disappearance of pensions and the tenuous state of Social Security continue to put more emphasis on that third leg of the stool—your own resources, saved and grown over your career. Though some lament the passing of the pensions, others point out that it is not such a bad thing that people have regained personal responsibility over their finances.

Pensions were predicated on the assumption that it was in the company's best interest for employees to stay put. To become vested in a pension required employees to demonstrate their allegiance to a single company, perhaps forgoing opportunities to advance their careers elsewhere. Pensions tied retirement security to long-term corporate loyalty. For some, the coming of the highly portable 401(k) meant freedom. It was a nest egg that they could take with them from one employer to the next.

Today, as part of one's retirement-income plan, we may need to recreate a pension for you when possible. A pension substitute of sorts, designed solely for you, and one that that cannot be taken away from you. A regular and lifelong stream of income that is not tied to your former employer, nor the solvency of a pension fund.

*We often utilize these strategies to
try to cover your day-to-day needs as
part of a multi-bucket income plan.
This then may allow us to position your
other assets in a manner as to keep
pace with inflation and to help you to
reach your other retirement goals.*

A fourth leg on the stool?

Another consideration for many retirees today is to add a so-called fourth leg to that wobbly stool to shore it up. Working part-time in retirement. Sometimes this is out of necessity and sometimes it is purely by choice. During this period following the Great Recession of 2008–2009, it is not uncommon for new clients that we meet with for the first time to want, or need, to incorporate another type of income resource into their plan: working part-time.

On the surface, some people may think: *If you are going to go back to work, why retire in the first place? I may not be able to earn as much as I do now anywhere else!* There is some logic in that, and we often address that with new clients. If your plan is to work in retirement, would it make more sense to delay your retirement date a few years and stay where you are? But for many, they may just be ready for a new chapter in their working life, or they are not physically or mentally able to continue in their current position. They may need to retire from their current position, but not from the workforce as a whole.

For others, the thought of completely stepping away from a position all at once is not in their DNA. They may feel they still have too much to accomplish at their current employer. They may want to retire gradually over an extended period of time. Some employers encourage this as a method to help mentor those that are going to fill that person's shoes. This new "semi-retiree" can act as both a mentor and a trainer for the new hire. A true win-win-win for the company, the new hire, and the retiree! This new part-time position also allows the new "retiree" to ease into his or her new life outside the workforce.

For others this "retirement work" is necessary to provide the resources needed to allow them to live and provide for their families. It is needed, and there is no other option. Part of our goal as retirement-income planners is to help folks work to avoid this type of situation. Sometimes it is unavoidable, and that is unfortunate. This, again, is why I encourage folks to start planning as early as possible. Part of our goal is to help you grow and position your resources in such a manner that working in retirement is a matter of choice, not a necessity.

We strive to look at the big picture. We work to craft an income stream from all your available resources, including Social Security and the proceeds from a 401(k), or IRA, and other investment accounts and income sources. We understand the serious responsibility that today's retirees face with the shift away from traditional pensions. You need to do this right. You will not have a second chance. You have no choice but to make this work for you.

I and my staff are here to help. I often tell people that I have retired a thousand times as I have worked with prospective retirees. Each time I have learned something new, something I can take with me to be of even better service to the next. I understand that you are only going to retire once. You may no longer have the three legged stool that your parents relied on, but you certainly will need a reliable place to rest.

CHAPTER 5

Your Coach, Your Team

"Each player on this team must do his one-eleventh!" That is the motto of one of the most successful football programs in NCAA Division II college football, the Northwest Missouri State University Bearcats of Maryville, Missouri. This system has served them well as they have won five NCAA Division II National Championships and fourteen conference championships over the past seventeen years. But they know it's not enough to only do your one-eleventh. Each coach and member of the team has to work in perfect concert with the others, following a game plan. Otherwise the players would just be heading out onto the field and scrambling in different directions without a goal in mind. They need a coach, a game plan to guide them, and they need a quarterback to initiate the plays and get things moving.

A qualified financial advisor serves as the coach and the quarterback for the financial game plan you work to implement. As a CFP® I serve in both capacities. I am a guide and a trainer for my clients, and

I help to hold them accountable for what they need to do, encouraging them to take action. The players bring many skills and talents to the field, but without coordination and teamwork, it might all be for nothing.

Qualified, trained, professional advisors help you with the big picture—not just the individual transactions as they come along. A true coach will have only your best interest at heart and will understand that an efficient and effective financial and retirement-income plan must be designed with your particular circumstances in mind. One size, or one plan, does not fit all!

That is the issue that often arises when people try to formulate their own financial plans based on information they glean from the media or the Internet. Those commentators and columnists know nothing about the individuals in the audience. It is presented as mass advice that may have little or no bearing on what might be best for you as an individual. To deal with your finances in that manner would be like trying to diagnose and treat yourself based upon what you saw watching an episode of the medical drama, *House*. It takes human understanding and careful consideration to provide the kind of care that brings results.

Like your doctor, your financial planner needs to sit down with you, eye to eye, and listen carefully as you describe your situation. And like your doctor, a financial planner can often provide the most value to you based on a long-standing relationship with you and your entire family. Your doctor knows your vital signs and has a record of your medical history, etc. That is essential background information needed for assessing your medical condition. Likewise, when you work with a qualified financial planner who has gathered your vital information—who took time to understand your family, your background, and your dreams—you can be much more confident that the advice provided should provide better results for your financial health as well.

None of the talking heads on television know anything about you or your personal situation. They often provide advice without any understanding of an individual's situation. How can a TV personality know what's best for you if he or she has never looked at your portfolio, or sat down with you for an in-depth talk about your goals or what is important to you? Qualified advisors will learn about you and your story, not just tell you theirs over the airwaves.

Nor can you find truly personalized service on the Internet. The web is an awesome source for general education and information. You can learn, for example, how a Roth IRA works, the details on various types of annuities, or you can brush up on the basic tools of estate planning. But that will not be sufficient to serve all the needs of you and your family. Again, it is information for the masses, and as such, it may not serve as suitable advice for you and your particular situation.

How about relatives, friends, and colleagues? They know you and your situation, don't they? True, they might seem to be trustworthy sources who have your best interests in mind, but remember that the choices that are good for them may be far from the ones that will be good for you. Their situation is not your situation, their goals are not your goals, and the plan that suits them could be disastrous for you. They may be in a different stage of life, with different family dynamics, and their tolerance for risk may be altogether different from yours. If you are sixty years old, that thirty-year-old nephew or coworker at the water cooler probably inhabits another world when it comes to financial matters. You need to do what is best for you and your family by working with a coach who understands *your* situation—someone working to execute a game plan just for you.

I hear it sometimes from soon-to-be retirees: "My buddy Tom retired last year, and here's what he did, so I'd like to do the same thing." Tom might be the same age, and he might have been born and raised in the same town and worked in the same industry. Still, that may mean little. What are Tom's goals for retirement? What is his family situation? What's important to him going forward? Until I learn a lot more about the individual, there is no way to know whether Tom's approach would make any sense for that person or not. I can't make that determination without getting to know that individual and hearing their story.

When people tell me about a tip that they heard on TV, I often remind them to remember that the media's agenda is not the same as theirs. The media's agenda is to capture attention, to boost audience share, and ultimately, to sell advertising. So the financial news often may tend toward sensationalizing. My goal is to gather unbiased information so that we can apply it to your particular circumstances based on good judgment.

A special relationship

I once was working with a young couple, talking about life insurance and a few other financial-planning issues, when at one point during the conversation, they looked at each other. "Should we tell him?" the wife asked the husband. "We probably need to tell him." And they did. They were expecting their first child—and they had yet to tell either set of their parents! Still, they realized that I needed to know this right away because it was central to the type of planning we were doing. I felt honored.

I have been a CERTIFIED FINANCIAL PLANNERTM professional since 2008. I agree that designations and certifications are only part of what makes a quality advisor, but my CFP® designation assures you of my fiduciary responsibility.

Insurance agents and stockbrokers are not always held to the fiduciary standard. Instead, they currently must only meet the suitability standard. Whatever they recommend must be suitable for the client, but that does not mean it is necessarily in the best interest of the client. As fiduciaries, CFP®s take an oath and an ethics pledge to always act in the best interest of their clients. It is what I am required to do, and I also believe that it is the right thing to do. When you do what is right for people, I believe it comes back to you twenty-fold.

To become a CFP® is to have reached a pinnacle of education in our profession. I had to complete and pass a course of study that included passing five four-hour exams, which then allowed me to qualify to sit for the CFP® National Board Exam. This exam took ten hours to complete over two days. On my exam date, only 49 percent of those who took the exam nationally passed, including those who were taking it for the second or third time. As a CFP®, I am also required stay up to date on practically all areas involving retirement and income planning and personal finance. These include, but are not limited to, changing tax laws, retirement plan rules, investment rules and trends, and estate planning rules. The continuing education requirements are substantial but necessary.

In my profession, you may see a variety of other designations after people's names, but you should realize that they are all NOT the same. There are only a few other certifications that require as high a level of testing and continuing education requirements as the CFP®. A Chartered Financial Consultant, designated as ChFC®, has stringent requirements as well, as do Certified Financial Analysts. CFAs are more geared toward the investment and fund-management side of our business. Individuals with this type of certification and education tend to work as fund managers, as well as financial planners.

"I have a CPA," people sometimes say, "and that's all I need." Oftentimes it may not be. CPAs are an essential member of a person's financial team, of course, and I work with CPAs all the time. But most are not trained as financial planners. Their expertise is primarily in tax analysis, which is a major consideration of the financial plan, but certainly not the only consideration. Sometimes, we have experienced where CPAs tend to see primarily through a tax lens. CPAs can be, and are, a great source of information and expertise. But every decision cannot be based solely on how it affects your tax situation. Many other factors come in to play, and that is why we feel you need a financial coach to help maintain the pr

As a CFP®, my goal is to be the quarterback and to work with those other team members who may include the CPA, perhaps an estate-planning attorney, a business attorney, an insurance specialist, and others. Who is on your team is going to be dictated by your particular situation.

Effective planning calls for a relationship that is open and caring and that doesn't happen overnight. When we meet with new clients, we realize that it takes time to build that comfort level. We respect that and realize that asking folks to share their personal information and life story with us is not easy, especially in the beginning. It comes through honestly caring and sharing life experiences. It comes not just from asking about someone's family and their goals, but also truly listening. A qualified advisor, frankly, often cares more about a client's financial situation than do many people who share that person's last name.

Unfortunately, some people associated with our industry use the term "financial planner" somewhat loosely. Many of those who use that title are not fiduciaries and may not do only what is suitable for the client—and that may also reflect what they find most *suitable for themselves* as well. Fortunately the Department of Labor has recently passed some rulings that are designed to help weed out unscrupulous "advisors" who are only in our industry to make a quick buck. These rules are designed to hold everyone to the standard of acting in a "fiduciary capacity." Time will tell how our industry will be changed by this new legislation.

Some of the pundits and talking heads on TV are often very critical of folks in our industry and try to lump us all together. Especially anyone who charges a commission for providing a financial product or service. I would like to point out that there is nothing wrong with utilizing products where the compensation is paid by way of commissions. In fact, they are the foundation of most all insurance-based products. To my knowledge, there is no other way to buy insurance. If you own a home or a car and have them insured, or ever even bought a pair of jeans at an upscale clothing store, guess what; you have paid commissions. It is an accepted business practice and part of doing commerce in our country.

I am not saying that either fee-based business or a commission-based model is necessarily better when it comes to working with a financial planner. What is important is that you know whom you are dealing with. In our business, we work on a fee-based model primarily, but we also work on commission as well. Nonetheless, as a fiduciary, regardless of how I receive compensation, I still have to do what is in the best interest of my clients. I have to be able to look in the mirror every day and know that I have done what was best for my clients.

A steadying hand

When considering your own finances, emotions may tend to run high, particularly in times of volatility when the media is often sensationalizing the story of the day. We believe you have to be able to see the forest for the trees, and somebody has to be the voice of reason. As your advisor, it is my responsibility to offer that voice. I understand why people get upset, and I am always ready to listen and talk about it. Never do I discount my clients' emotions and concerns, but I do my best to help them reason things through.

Touchy issues sometimes arise during the course of working with folks. Everyone reacts differently to what they hear on the news, and sometimes they may be on the verge of making a rash decision. Often what they need to do, first and foremost, is to see the big picture. I work to make sure that they look at their situation in context and from the proper perspective. I try to offer a steadying hand to help guide their ship. To keep the big picture in mind.

I believe that when you are considering whom to hire as your financial planner, the integrity and likability of that person should be major considerations.

Are you dealing with someone who looks you in the eye? Someone who is really listening to you? Someone you can relate to? Do you feel that you will continue to get along with that person and their firm as the years go by? Consider the Canoe Test. Ask yourself, "If you were canoeing across a big lake with this person and you lost the paddles and had to sit with them for several hours, could you do it? Could you talk to this person? Could you rely on this person to help keep you calm if the waters got rough? Is this someone you could work with to devise a plan to get through your current situation? Could you rely on them to help you? Or would they just work to save themselves? You must choose wisely when considering a co-captain for your voyage!

In this technological age, I sometimes find myself offering a virtual handshake and looking clients in the eye via a teleconference. I have a few clients with whom our relationship has been primarily via the telephone and/or a computer monitor, and yet, even then, I strive to connect personally. As long as technology allows the personal touch, even across the miles, it is serving us well. Our office is in a relatively small town, but as of this writing, I have investment clients in twenty-one states and insurance clients in twenty-two states. Technology opens the possibility for a worldwide reach—and that's wonderful, so long as we treat each other as if we were only a handshake and a smile away from each other. When we utilize technology in our office to maintain and grow long-distance relationships with our clients, it is paramount that we provide the same level of service and practice the same values of honesty and integrity as if they were across the table from us.

I know that I am not the best advisor who ever walked the earth. But I do know that I am a good listener, and I care about people and can relate to them. That, I believe, is what matters most. I have no hidden agenda. What you see is what you get. I'm a big guy—six feet four and 290 pounds—so if I had a gruff personality, I'm sure a lot of folks might head for the hills! Maybe that's why all my life I have done my best to cultivate a friendly demeanor. But I genuinely care about my clients, and that's what you need in the advisor you choose to work with. You want someone with a genuine interest in you, your family, and your long-term goals. He or she will have a lot to do with the course of your family's financial future. So, please choose wisely.

CHAPTER 6

Managing the Risks

Almost everything I do as a financial planner in some way involves managing risks. They can come at you from every direction. As we work with our clients, we strive to find ways to help mitigate those risks in your financial and retirement-income plans.

During the 2008–2009 economic crisis, unfortunately a lot of people panicked. As they saw their account values falling, they succumbed to fear that they would lose even more. As they listened to the media, they imagined their retirement dreams spiraling down the drain. Some pulled out their investments at precisely the wrong time, when the market hit bottom and they could not stand the uncertainty anymore. They sold low—and then many stayed on the sidelines in fear as the market rebounded.

So could have anything have been done? Some folks might have limited that risk if they had had strategies in place before the crisis and the confidence that their life savings would be protected. Having a plan might have assured them that they would not run out of money in the foreseeable future and that their lifestyle would remain intact. They would not have felt the panic that drove many of them to pull up stakes and bail out of the market. Sound and thorough planning is one critical element to managing risk, whether that threat comes from the market itself or from the very human tendency to overreact.

History has shown that to be true, time and time again. In the precipitous stock market plunge of 1929, investors were not just jumping in mass out of the market; a few of them were actually jumping out of windows. With financial planning, you strive to not be caught by surprise. Your goal is to look at the contingencies and the possible scenarios and as many of the "what ifs" as possible You strive to have a clear picture of an income plan that will help see you through your retirement days.

And what may come your way involves much more than what the market might do, although that is the risk that people usually think of first when considering the threats to their portfolio. There are a variety of other risks, such as the toll that inflation can take on your purchasing power and how fluctuating interest rates could upset your retirement expectations. They all hold the power to significantly influence your financial well-being.

In this chapter, we will take a look at some of those risks, starting with a closer look at what investors face in the market. In upcoming chapters, we will look even more closely at two particular risks: the toll of taxation and the possible prospect of needing protection against the effects of long-term elderly disability (a.k.a., long-term care).

Market risk

Many people, when making their investment decisions, may primarily look at the average annual return that a particular investment has provided over a certain period of time. Be careful. That average return does not tell the whole story. You may need to consider the sequence of those returns from year to year. Virtually any investment will have some years that win and some years that lose. The big question is which comes first—and whether you will be withdrawing money from your portfolio during those down times.

During your accumulation days, when you are building a portfolio that will remain untouched until retirement, that sequence of returns is not as important. I am not saying that it doesn't matter, but if you are not drawing upon your portfolio for income, then you are able to leave it alone so that it can recover from short-term market volatility. Historically, the market has invariably recovered, and the long-term trend has been positive. History has shown this to be the reliable pattern, even during recessions, depressions, and world wars. But please also be aware that we cannot predict the future performance of the financial markets based upon past performance.

Accumulation phase

During your accumulation years, as long as no withdrawals are taken from a portfolio, sequence of returns has no effect on performance.

	Portfolio A		Portfolio B	
	EARLY LOSSES		EARLY GAINS	
AGE	% RETURN	ACCT. VALUE	% RETURN	ACCT. VALUE
51		$500,000		$500,000
52	-23.1%	$384,474	22.7%	$613,500
53	-6.1%	$360,923	19.6%	$733,960
54	-0.3%	$359,953	18.0%	$866,366
55	24.5%	$448,028	24.5%	$1,078,350
56	18.0%	$528,852	-0.3%	$1,075,454
57	19.6%	$632,691	-6.1%	$1,009,577
58	22.7%	$776,312	-23.1%	$776,312
59	-23.1%	$596,943	22.7%	$952,535
60	-6.1%	$560,377	19.6%	$1,345,140
61	-0.3%	$558,872	18.0%	$1,674,272
62	24.5%	$695,618	24.5%	$1,669,775
63	18.0%	$821,107	-0.3%	$1,567,493
64	19.6%	$982,331	-6.1%	$1,567,493
65	22.7%	$1,205,320	-23.1%	$1,205,320
	6.5% Average	$1,205,320 Total	6.5% Average	$1,205,320 Total

*The returns and values indicated are hypothetical in nature and are for illustrative purposes only.

It's an entirely different story, however, if you are withdrawing money from your portfolio at the same time that it is hit by a bear market. In this situation, your portfolio can suffer some devastating consequences.

Income distribution phase

During your income distribution years, sequence of returns may have a major impact on the long-term success of a portfolio.

Annual Income Example:

Starting value for both portfolios: $1,000,000

Annual income withdrawals: 5 percent of first year account value, adjusted by 3.5 percent inflation each year thereafter

	Portfolio A				Portfolio B		
	EARLY LOSSES				EARLY GAINS		
AGE	% RETURN	WITHDRAWAL	ACCT. VALUE		% RETURN	WITHDRAWAL	ACCT. VALUE
65			$1,000,000				$1,000,000
66	-23.1%	$50,000	$730,500		22.7%	$50,000	$1,165,650
67	-6.1%	$51,750	$637,173		19.6%	$51,750	$1,332,613
68	-0.3%	$53,561	$582,045		18.0%	$53,561	$1,509,792
69	24.5%	$55,436	$655,461		24.5%	$55,436	$1,810,211
70	18.0%	$57,376	$705,978		-0.3%	$57,376	$1,748,127
71	19.6%	$59,384	$773,552		-6.1%	$59,384	$1,585,299
72	22.7%	$61,463	$873,733		-23.1%	$61,463	$1,171,750
80	-23.1%	$80,935	$316,735		22.7%	$80,935	$1,538,381
81	-6.1%	$83,767	$218,697		19.6%	$83,767	$1,740,225
82	-0.3%	$86,699	$131,643		18.0%	$86,699	$1,951,820
83	24.5%	$89,734	$52,164		24.5%	$89,734	$2,317,706
84	18.0%	$52,164	$0		-0.3%	$92,874	$2,218,856
85	19.6%	$0	$0		-6.1%	$96,125	$1,992,703
86	22.7%	$0	$0		-23.1%	$99,489	$1,455,782
94	-23.1%	$0	$0		22.7%	$131,009	$1,650,179
95	-6.1%	$0	$0		19.6%	$135,594	$1,811,973
96	-0.3%	$0	$0		18.0%	$140,340	$1,973,194
97	24.5%	$0	$0		24.5%	$145,252	$2,275,208
98	18.0%	$0	$0		-0.3%	$150,335	$2,119,166
99	19.6%	$0	$0		-6.1%	$155,597	$1,843,290
100	22.7%	$0	$0		-23.1%	$161,043	$1,293,560
	6.5%	$1,277,148	$0		6.5%	$3,333,701	$1,293,560
	Average	Total Withdrawals	Ending Value		Average	Total Withdrawals	Total

*The returns and values indicated are hypothetical in nature and are for illustrative purposes only.

You can never count on the market moving in a straight line. It seldom works that way. Instead, it usually rises and falls in cycles. If you are caught on the wrong side of those cycles, it can be very troublesome. Yes, the market average over the years has been somewhat impressive, but it might not be impressive for you. The average annual return of the Standard & Poor's 500 index since its inception in 1928 has been around 10 percent, not accounting for inflation. But folks who retired in 1965 saw nothing like those returns for fifteen years. And if you retired in 1980, you likewise were in for a sustained period of disappointment.

It may be very difficult to recover financially if a few bad years strike the market right as you retire and begin withdrawing from your portfolio. A decade later, your average annual returns might seem healthy enough, and yet your portfolio may have taken a substantial hit. Let's say you could shift the sequence of those returns so that the good years came first and the bad ones at the end. Your portfolio may be in far better shape than if the years came vice versa. However, in either scenario, the average return for the decade would be exactly the same.

Occasionally someone will ask me, "I see that this particular mutual fund has been averaging X percent, so can I get that next year?" And here is my answer: I don't know. The average return tells you very little. It is only a measure of broad performance over an extended period of time. If you are looking to get that return in a given year, your guess is as good as mine if that investment will deliver it. Over the long term, based on historical performance, it appears that those types of returns may be possible. But, the long term is not one year.

To make your investment decisions based on averages is a perilous strategy. To counteract that sequence-of-return risk, we sometimes use tools that are designed to help ease that anxiety. We may use strategies that include annuities or laddered bonds, for example, in order to maintain a reliable and consistent income stream during volatile times. I will explain in chapter 8 how to use such strategies to help keep the sequence-of-return threat at a minimum. We will look at ways that may help you be able to participate in the market without potential volatility wrecking your portfolio's ability to provide retirement income.

Some investors proudly proclaim how much they may have beat the index, but are congratulations really in order if the index falls 30 percent and their portfolio only falls 28 percent? Technically, this is a win because we know it is easier to move forward if we don't fall back as much as the market index did. But often folks don't feel that it's a win, and I get that. Even though they beat the market average, it's still a loss to them.

I, like every other financial advisor, have had to console clients on occasion during volatile times when their portfolios show decline. Nobody ever likes to lose money, but it is part of the normal equity-market cycle. My goal is to help clients limit those losses and have a plan in place so that those losses, either short or long term, do not wreck their retirement-income plan.

Some of the pundits out there would tell you, "Just invest in an index fund. You'll do just as well." That's not always so. When you look at different market sectors and strategies and work with an advisor, you may be able to add value beyond just riding out an index fund.

For the individual investor, the concept of rebalancing the portfolio is often fundamental to success. Without it, you can also experience what is known as "style drift." Let's say, for example, that you assess your risk tolerance and decide up front that you want a portfolio that is 60 percent bonds and 40 percent stocks, although you might have a variety of asset classes. Over time, if you make no adjustments to your portfolio, those percentages may start to get out of balance. If your stocks increase in value year after year, they eventually will claim a larger portion of the total portfolio, and you might find yourself with a fifty-fifty mix, or even 40 percent bonds and 60 percent stocks.

That now exposes you to more risk than you originally intended, and so you need to rebalance to get back to your original allocation. If you do not, you will be fine as long as the market is rising. But when it turns downward, as it inevitably will, now 60 percent of your portfolio will be susceptible to equity-market risk, instead of 40 percent.

In other words, you may need to do a bit of harvesting as some of your asset classes do better than others. You may need to do something that is rather counterintuitive. You may need to take away from your winners and give to those that have been losing in value. Remember your original objectives and the level of risk that you deemed appropriate to govern your overall plan.

We leave it up to our clients how often they want to rebalance their portfolios. We suggest rebalancing at least annually, but generally, we suggest rebalancing semi-annually. Some clients are tempted to ride their stocks ever higher when they are doing well. But we work to help our clients understand that they should stay true to the risk tolerance established in their investment-policy statement.

Purchasing-power risk

Think about what it would cost to replace the tires on your car today. Then think about what you paid for new tires twenty years ago. You might not have imagined the price would go up so much! Now, imagine what you will be paying for new tires twenty years from now. My guess is that the cost will be higher than you predict.

> *In most cases, it is essential that you take purchasing-power risk into account when projecting your retirement income needs into the decades ahead.*

Some people entering retirement become so conservative in their ways that they want to take all of the growth potential out of their portfolio. I certainly understand the instinct to protect what you have worked so hard to accumulate. Nonetheless, you can be certain that the toll that inflation can take on your ability to buy goods and services in the future will not cease. Based upon historical norms, in the future, your current lifestyle will inevitably cost more to maintain. Your purchasing power slowly but surely will dwindle, and you will need a higher income to live the lifestyle that you do today.

"I just want to keep my money in the bank because at least there's no risk there," folks sometimes tell me. Unfortunately, they are only thinking about principle risk when they take that stance. The risk that you face in leaving all of your money in the bank, with little growth potential, is sort of like an error of omission. By doing nothing, you and your portfolio may get left behind. Sure, you will be protecting your money from principle risk. But the time will come when you need to buy a full set of tires, and you may only be able to afford two. Maybe just one. After all, today it is not uncommon to live thirty years or more in retirement.

Think of other items that you commonly purchase today. What did they cost twenty years ago, what do they cost today, and what do you expect that they will cost in the future? If you earn half a percent at the bank on your money, you simply will not keep up with inflation. That will be the case even in a normal inflationary environment. And if inflation, heaven forbid, were to get out of hand and rise to double digits—think back to the Jimmy Carter and Gerald Ford days—your savings could be left in the dust. True, you likely will earn somewhat more on your bank account or certificate of deposit, but throughout history, those rates have never kept pace with inflation.

So what is a retiree to do? The clear answer is that your nest egg, or at least a portion of it, needs the potential to grow at least enough to keep pace with inflation so that your purchasing power remains intact. Generally, that will mean that a portion of your portfolio may need some exposure to the equities market. However, that does not mean that you will need to fear that your income stream will dry up. You may be able to arrange your portfolio so that a portion of it produces a reliable immediate income to support your lifestyle, while also riding the market higher with plenty of time to recover if the economy turns south. We will take a closer look at retirement income strategies in chapter eight.

Interest-rate risk

If long ago you had based your retirement security upon the once-impressive rates that you could get on CDs, you certainly would be suffering today. Forty years ago, my grandfather used to say that he was making enough interest on his bank CDs that he could afford to trade in his car for a new one every year. If he could see the price of cars today and how low the rates on those CDs have sunk, I know he would be surprised and very disappointed.

When your income depends primarily upon interest rates derived from the market place, you are dealing with interest-rate risk. If you were expecting to get 5 percent for years on end and now find yourself getting less than 1 percent, your retirement resources may grow to a fraction of what you anticipated.

Interest-rate risk is a major concern for CD and bond investors. Bond values fall as interest rates rise and vice versa. The fixed-rate bonds that investors already hold will fall in price if newer investments with more attractive, higher rates enter the market. Likewise, investors can expect their bonds to rise in price if the newer investments come with less-attractive interest rates. However, as of this writing (2016), since interest rates have been at historical lows for several years, which way do you expect that they will trend in the years ahead? Nobody can say for sure, but it is the question that is front and center for many bond investors.

Longevity risk

This is the risk that you might live too long—or rather, that you might outlive your money. Were it not for longevity risk, many of the other risks would not exist. Inflation would be a moot issue, since we would not live long enough to see its effect. The Social Security system's troubles would be over, since retirees would not be around long to collect benefits. Certainly it would be far less likely that you would have to enter a nursing home, which could potentially eat away at your resources.

Today many people expect to remain healthy and active for decades after they leave the workforce. On one hand, that is to be applauded. On the other hand, it creates a huge responsibility on each individual and our society as a whole. We now need to provide for ourselves longer than ever before in history. How are we as a society to address this? On a broad level, it likely will mean changes to entitlement programs. On the individual level at which I work with clients, it means building a portfolio that is not entirely at the mercy of forces they cannot control, such as fluctuating markets and interest rates.

Statistics show that people have begun to enjoy lengthy retirements that may potentially last longer than the span of their working years. They have no intention of passing away a few years into retirement, as many of their great-grandparents did. With advances in healthcare and lifestyle, you, or your spouse, easily could live past the hundred-year mark. You need to be ready for that.

You may need to accumulate the necessary resources during your working years, to sustain your desired lifestyle for way longer than you ever imagined.

That is the gist of everything we are covering in this book.

The risk of yourself

Many of the actions that people take in life are based upon early experiences, which may include false beliefs about money. We are also, to a large extent, creatures who follow the herd. Human beings often do things because everyone else is doing them and feel safety in numbers.

It is unfortunate, but undeniable, that fear and greed are two fundamental driving factors in many decisions that we make. When you combine that with the follow-the-herd mentality, you can see how so many are led astray in their investment and financial-planning lives.

Fear sometimes gets in the way of logic. People become scared about things that they do not fully understand. Compounding the problem is the bad press that the financial services industry has received over the past few years. Most people do not know what a true financial planner even does. The term is used loosely, and sometimes by people who take advantage. Then the public hears a bunch of media accounts about the Bernie Madoffs of the world, and cynicism sets in. Good news doesn't sell. Bad news does. It's that simple. Have you ever come across a story in the mainstream media about a financial advisor helping somebody plan a thirty-year retirement that meets their goals and fulfills their dreams? Unfortunately, no.

I believe that folks need to acknowledge that their own human behavior may pose a serious risk to their own situation. Investors can overreact or underreact, based on feelings of the day or even of the moment. Caught up in the sensationalism of the media, sometimes they can make precisely the wrong decision. With the guidance of a qualified advisor who focuses on the facts and how they apply to your personal situation, you can hopefully rise above the noise and make decisions based upon logic and your own long-term goals.

CHAPTER 7

Tax Strategies

The comedian Henny Youngman, king of the one-liners, once quipped that he was proud to be paying taxes in America—but he could be just as proud by paying half as much!

I remember a professor in one of my college economics classes explaining the difference between tax evasion and tax avoidance. Only the first is bad, and you can go to jail for it. The latter is perfectly legitimate. In fact, some provisions within the tax code encourage it. We should strive for it whenever possible. I believe Mr. Youngman would have approved!

In any event, to be paying taxes usually means you are making money. "There are worse things than having to pay taxes," he used to say. I remember as a young man my father pointing that out to me. That doesn't mean you should be paying any more than you are required to. It just means that if you have made a legitimate living and are required to pay income taxes, you certainly can be proud to be a productive and contributing citizen.

He used to also say, "Tax management is critical, but you usually can't spend yourself rich," and I understand his point. To prepay and buy business assets for tax purposes can be a great strategy, and it's one I have used myself many times—but what he was saying is that you should not do so solely for the tax break. Those should be necessary expenses. Necessary assets or inputs that you need. Nonetheless, the government gives us tax breaks for good reason: to encourage certain behaviors, such as saving for retirement and purchasing and owning a home. It certainly is not unpatriotic, or illegal, to take advantage of every tax break available.

Tax management is a major part of the work we do. One of our goals is to help our clients find the tax savings available to them. It is often said that it is not so much what you earn, but what you get to keep that matters. Saving on taxes amounts to resources you can now direct elsewhere. Unmanaged taxation can eat away at your portfolio and your retirement savings. Usually the damage comes slowly. It's not a dramatic event, in most cases; instead, the money leaks away year after year over your lifetime. Most folks are not tax experts, so this may potentially go on unnoticed for years. But oftentimes there are steps you can take to help manage this liability. We, along with the guidance of your tax professional, may be able to help toward that end.

Tax diversification

From a tax perspective, the assets within your portfolio will be basically one of three types: they will either be subject to taxation immediately, subject to taxation somewhere down the road, or never subject to taxation. In short: taxable, tax deferred, or tax-free.

Each of those may be important for a well-functioning portfolio. But, your investment decisions during your accumulation years, as well as during your retirement income-planning years, cannot be driven solely by how the assets will be taxed. However, that does need to be a consideration.

All three types of investments are good, and all three of them may be bad. In other words, they are all viable choices depending on how they are positioned in the portfolio. They must be used in the correct manner and for the correct purposes. Used correctly in your retirement-income plan, they can all be very beneficial. Used incorrectly, they may be of little benefit, or potentially harmful to a plan. That is particularly true during the distribution of resources for retirement income and estate planning, as I will explain in later chapters. There likely will be a place for all three types of accounts in your planning, and that is the principle of tax diversification.

Taxable investments are those on which you must pay income tax for the year that they provide you with earnings. Many assets are within this category, including stocks and their dividends, treasury bonds, mutual funds, and certificates of deposit. Tax-free investments, which can grow without future tax consequences, include the Roth IRA (when utilized correctly) and municipal bonds, as well as 529 education accounts and some insurance products. Tax-deferred investments include the 401(k) and similar retirement plans, traditional IRAs, and a variety of tax-deferred annuities.

Tax-deferral considerations

The Traditional IRA, 401(k), and similar tax-qualified retirement plans have helped a lot of people build their funds for retirement. They are a tool, just as a Roth IRA is a tool, or any other investment vehicle for that matter. They must be used wisely and correctly. To the greatest extent possible, you should strive to use them for your own benefit, rather than that of Uncle Sam.

These retirement plans are designed to accumulate on a tax-deferred basis while you are working, with the presumption that you will be in a lower tax bracket when the day comes where you begin to withdraw those assets—either voluntarily at any point after you turn fifty-nine-and-a-half years old, or as a required minimum distribution (RMD) each year after you turn seventy and a half. You don't want to forget about those required minimum distributions. If you do not take them out, you will be assessed a penalty of 50 percent of the amount you should have withdrawn.

Recent income tax rates have been low compared to historical levels. That raises the question as to whether they will stay low, especially considering the amount of national debt that our country now carries. In other words, does it make sense to defer all of the taxes on your investments until later? This is one consideration when putting together a retirement-income plan.

Let there be no mistake: when it comes to your tax-deferred retirement plans, Uncle Sam is still patiently waiting. When you turn seventy and a half, even if you don't need the money that has been growing in your 401(k) or IRA, the government will want its share of tax revenue from it. The IRS rules force you to begin withdrawing from your nest egg and paying the long-delayed tax upon it. It is possible that you may be deferring your taxes to a higher rate than what you would pay today. Depending upon your situation, you may want to consider some alternative strategies.

One approach is an arbitrage strategy utilizing a life insurance policy in conjunction with your tax-deferred retirement plan. This can make sense if you have a considerable amount of money in your retirement accounts and you will not need it all for income, you are insurable, and your intention is to leave the money to your beneficiaries. To utilize this strategy, you would withdraw your RMD, pay the required tax, and then use a good portion of the remaining proceeds to pay a premium each year on a life insurance policy. Your children would get a potentially tax-free death benefit that probably would be much larger than their inheritance otherwise would have been due to the leverage provided by the life insurance policy. If they were simply to receive only the 401(k) account, they probably would pay a significant amount of tax on their total proceeds. The insurance payout goes to them tax-free. This strategy is not suitable for everyone, but it can be an effective tax-advantaged method to leverage assets that are designated to be left for your heirs. Of course, you must also be insurable for this type of strategy to work.

IRA RMD – life insurance arbitrage strategy

Example parameters:

- A married, seventy-and-a-half-year-old client with $400,000 IRA does not want all of it for income.
- He wishes to leave as much as possible to his heirs in the most tax-efficient manner.
- He is a nonsmoker in good health—making him insurable for life insurance at the preferred underwriting class.
- His assumed life expectancy is age eighty-five.

- Assume a hypothetical rate of return on his investment of 6 percent annually.*
- Required minimum distributions (RMD) are taken on Jan. 1 each year.
- Utilize the uniform life-expectancy table for RMDs.
- Assume 25 percent of each payment must go to taxes.
- There is a life insurance premium of $10,000 per year.
- The remaining portion of each RMD, after taxes and life insurance premiums, is used for increasing living expenses.

AGE IRA BALANCE FACTOR RMD

YEAR	OWNER AGE	IRA BALANCE	FACTOR	RMD
2016	69	$400,000.00		$0.00
2017	70	$424,000.00	27.4	$15,474.45
2018	71	$433,965.55	26.5	$16,376.06
2019	72	$443,627.42	25.6	$17,329.20
2020	73	$452,915.87	24.7	$18,336.67
2021	74	$461,754.15	23.8	$19,401.43
2022	75	$470,057.97	22.9	$20,526.55
2023	76	$477,734.90	22	$21,715.22
2024	77	$484,683.77	21.2	$22,862.44
2025	78	$490,902.36	20.3	$24,182.38
2026	79	$496,174.12	19.5	$25,444.83
2027	80	$500,499.74	18.7	$26,764.69
2028	81	$503,765.03	17.9	$28,143.30
2029	82	$505,847.63	17.1	$29,581.73
2030	83	$506,616.76	16.3	$31,080.78
2031	84	$505,932.99	15.5	$32,640.84
2032	85	$503,648.13	14.8	$34,030.02

*Assumes a hypothetical return of 6 percent annually. Utilized for illustrative purposes only. Not representative of any investment or product. Utilized Uniform Life Expectancy table for RMD calculations.

Paying a life insurance premium of about $10,000 per year, a seventy-year-old male, nonsmoker, preferred underwriting class, utilizing an A-plus rated insurance carrier in our current marketplace, could anticipate to be able to acquire somewhere between $300,000 to $400,000 of permanent death benefit from this policy. Based upon current law, heirs should be able to receive the death benefit from this policy tax-free!

Instead of buying the life insurance, if you were to reinvest that same $10,000/year in a taxable account earning 6 percent, paying capital gains taxes out of the account each year at 15 percent, you could anticipate to have built up about $245,000 at age eighty-five, after taxes, to leave to your heirs. (See the following chart).

YEAR PROJECTED BALANCE PROJECTED AFTER TAXES PROJECTED DEATH BENEFIT PAYABLE

YEAR	BALANCE	AFTER TAXES	DEATH BENEFIT
2017	$10,318	$10,270	*$343,000
2018	$21,255	$21,064	*$343,000
2019	$32,848	$32,408	*$343,000
2020	$45,137	$44,331	*$343,000
2021	$58,163	$56,862	*$343,000
2022	$71,971	$70,032	*$343,000
2023	$86,607	$83,874	*$343,000
2024	$102,122	$98,421	*$343,000
2025	$118,567	$113,711	*$343,000
2026	$135,999	$129,780	*$343,000
2027	$154,477	$146,669	*$343,000
2028	$174,064	$164,419	*$343,000
2029	$194,825	$183,074	*$343,000
2030	$216,833	$202,681	*$343,000
2031	$240,161	$223,288	*$343,000
2032	$264,889	$244,946	*$343,000

*Assumes a hypothetical return of 6 percent annually and a capital gains rate of 15 percent. Utilized for illustrative purposes only. Not representative of any investment or product. Projected *$343,000 permanent death benefit utilized is based upon the projected benefit from an A+ rated carrier currently available in our marketplace at the time of this writing.

KEY POINTS/OPPORTUNITIES OF UTILIZING THE ARBITRAGE STRATEGY:

✓ Proceeds of life insurance pass to beneficiaries tax-free.

✓ Proceeds of life policy pass to beneficiaries outside of the expense and delays of the probate process.

✓ After coverage is established and all requirements are met, the full proceeds of the life policy are paid out regardless of when the policy owner dies. This could be at age eighty-five as projected, later, or earlier due to premature death.

✓ Life insurance death benefit proceeds would be in addition to the remaining taxable IRA balance that would be left to your heirs.

✓ If only reinvesting the unused portion of the RMD as illustrated above, unless positioned properly, this amount could be subject to the expense and delays of the probate process.

✓ Net amount of proceeds passed to beneficiaries may be increased substantially by leveraging the benefits of a life insurance policy in this arbitrage strategy.

*This example and all of the information provided is for illustrative purposes only. This example was provided to illustrate the concept of this type of strategy and is not representative of any particular investment type, policy, or contract. The growth rate of 6 percent was for illustrative purposes and does not reflect the anticipated or promised return of any certain type of investment, policy, or contract. Assumes current tax and capital gains rates. This strategy is not applicable or suitable for everyone. You should consult with your tax preparer, your financial advisor, and your insurance professional to see if this strategy is right for your situation.

Always consider the best timing for using tax-deferred retirement assets. If you need them for income, when should you turn that cash flow on? Does it make sense to keep waiting until you are forced to withdraw your money in your seventies, at which point your account may have grown to a point that those withdrawals lift you into a higher tax bracket? And consider this: at that point, you will probably be receiving your Social Security, and much of that benefit could become taxable due to those 401(k) and IRA required minimum distributions. In some instances, it may be a far better strategy to start withdrawing more of your 401(k) or IRA money earlier to cover living expenses, postponing your Social Security benefit and allowing it to grow. The goal with this type of strategy is to reduce your total taxable income bill while also creating a larger survivors' Social Security benefit for the surviving spouse.

Here's another example of a strategy we may employ: Sometimes we find that people may have tax-deferred annuities with a guaranteed minimum-income benefit that was put in place on annuities purchased before the market correction of 2008–2009. Of course, the market has recovered considerably since then, but because of how those contract riders were designed, some of the income rider benefit values are much larger than the actual value of the annuity.

In such cases, we may find that it makes sense to go ahead and turn on that annuity and put it to use. Let's say, for example, it's a twenty-year pay-out annuity. Part of the income would be used to pay the required taxes, and part of it could be used to purchase a twenty-year premium pay life insurance policy. The result is that the annuity payout has now been leveraged into a tax-free benefit for the heirs.

These types of strategies are not for everyone. It is important that all of the stars are in alignment for these to be utilized. You would need to be insurable, for example, and this would have to be income that you would not otherwise need for living expenses.

Again, with all strategies, we need to consider many factors, including tax consequences. Sometimes clients have told me that since they are required to take money out of their 401(k)s or IRAs and they don't need it, perhaps they should just move it into a CD or some other taxable investment. "I want to keep it safe," they will explain. Yes, that might protect the principal, but they are not keeping their money safe against inflation risk and taxes. They will be paying the deferred tax hit upon distribution of that money, and then they will be taxed again on its growth in a CD. So not only will they be taxed twice, but the growth on that investment may be insufficient to keep up with inflation.

Roth conversions

Some people take the approach of converting a portion of their tax-deferred retirement funds into a Roth IRA, paying part of the tax bill up front so that it will not all be taxed later. There are a variety of considerations to weigh before deciding whether that strategy is right for you, and we can help to step you through those.

A Roth conversion can be an estate-planning strategy, for example, for people who cannot qualify for life insurance in an arbitrage strategy. The Roth tax classification currently does not require required minimum distribution. Children receiving Roth assets will need to withdraw the money because they cannot leave it in the account in perpetuity. But, even when they do so, they will not be required to report it on their income taxes. I sometimes tell them that if their 401(k) or IRA money is intended primarily as a bequest to their kids, they may want to consider a Roth conversion earlier as opposed to later. They should not wait until they are seventy-and-a-half years old. Again, it all comes down to what you get to keep, or what your children get to keep.

When transferring money into a Roth, you pay the taxes at the time of the conversion. First, you roll over your 401(k) assets, or a portion of them, into an IRA. Then, when you convert that account to a Roth, the money within it becomes fully taxable. You will receive a form 1099 for that amount, and it will be part of your taxable income for that year.

From that point forward, you have a Roth IRA to which you may be able to contribute every year if you qualify. As with any IRA, you must have earned income to be able to contribute to it. You cannot put in money from your pension, for example. Nor can you simply transfer your required minimum distribution into a Roth. People ask me all the time whether that can be done. Sorry, but Uncle Sam wants you to pay your taxes on it first. If you are older than fifty-nine and a half, and still working and earning a wage, you can take a distribution while also investing the equivalent amount of dollars in your Roth. But, you cannot do a direct rollover to that account.

The takeaway here is that if you are going to start a conversion, you may want to begin early. Get your plan in place, and work with someone who understands the steps required. It may be beneficial to do the conversion systematically over time. In other words, spread out the tax burden over more than one year. The money that you convert will become fully taxable in that year, so you may want to do this gradually. When we work out retirement-income plans for clients, we compare a variety of scenarios to figure out the approach and the timing that may make the most sense for them. This requires a close look at the big picture. Some might benefit if they begin a Roth conversion and start paying some tax now, thereby later reducing the amount of their required distributions and possibly reducing the taxable portion of their Social Security benefit, as I mentioned previously.

Stretch provision

When an IRA owner dies and the proceeds are bequeathed to someone other than their spouse, the beneficiary is classified as a non-spousal beneficiary. The beneficiary of a non-spousal IRA always may exercise the option of cashing out an inherited IRA and paying the tax on the lump sum. However, as of this writing, the IRA allows you to set up another option: the beneficiary can stretch out distributions from that IRA over his or her lifetime. That also stretches out the tax deferral for many more years. This is a strategy that may allow that money to grow without taxation for several generations.

Unfortunately, the stretch provision is not utilized as often as it perhaps should be. This strategy requires a sense of patience and delayed gratification from the next generation. A patience that is very difficult for many of these beneficiaries. Often we see the recipients of these accounts wanting to utilize the money right away.

When leaving IRA assets to your children, you cannot require them to exercise the stretch provision. You certainly can suggest it, but when you are gone, they will have the option of taking the IRA proceeds however they prefer. They can set up the stretch on their own, but you might wish to facilitate that possibility by making arrangements with your financial planner before your passing.

If you want your children to stretch their IRA inheritance, it is important to clearly communicate to them in advance that such a thing is possible and that it may be in their best interest. Let them know that even a modest amount of money, if handled correctly, may become a sizable treasure for the family in a few generations. Otherwise, that potential for a wonderful legacy could be lost if they decide to spend the money on an immediate need, or desire, of the moment. You may have devoted years to saving that money, so you may wish to communicate clearly and promptly how you expect it to be managed.

Unfortunately, often we also see beneficiaries take the money as a lump sum unaware of the pending tax consequences. If there is any stretch period utilized, it is usually over a very short time. The heirs often seem to lack the patience for a longer stretch. And sometimes they spend all of the IRA funds without withholding anything back for the taxes. This is one of many reasons why we encourage our clients to involve their children in their planning process. This is especially critical in the later years when estate planning with adult children becomes a major consideration.

The right strategy for you

Throughout history our tax codes has provided tax breaks to encourage investment. When entrepreneurs pursue opportunities, they work to increase the bottom line, which in turn allows them to hire more people, build more products, and stimulate the economy. The ultimate goal of our economy is to promote industry.

For individuals, likewise, tax breaks put more money in their pockets so they, too, can spend more and stimulate the economy. It's not that the government doesn't need the money; to the contrary, the goal is to bring more money into the government's coffers via economic growth. In addition, by promoting desirable activities and behaviors, the government saves money. The government need not pay for certain services when it can encourage private enterprise, through tax breaks, to provide them. It also encourages donations to charity, for example, through tax exemptions.

Although the tax code provides such opportunities, Uncle Sam does not knock on your door and offer to explain it all to you. It's up to you to figure it out, and/or to work with someone who thoroughly understands your situation and can help determine the right approach for you.

I am not a tax professional, and I am not licensed to give tax advice. But as a CFP®, I am required to understand our tax code fairly well. I am required to understand how taxes may affect the income from your investments, and how tax-qualified savings plans work. Part of my job as an advisor is to also help you to get in touch with precisely the right professionals you need depending upon your situation. Think of it as an investment, not an expense, to work with a tax professional. It is often money well spent that may put money back in your pocket.

When it comes to tax matters, the team approach is often best. The CPA is not going to know about everything in your life. He or she may not be privy to your other investments and your personal situation and therefore may not have a clear picture of what you may be able to use to offset your taxable gains. For example, many people suffered losses in 2008 and 2009, and they perhaps could have used the opportunity to "harvest" those losses by selling certain assets to keep taxes down. Your financial planner needs to be working with your CPA to be sure that you are taking advantage of these type of tax-harvesting opportunities.

I strive to look at the big picture. Your tax professional will work to make a determination on taxes, but you need a coordinator for your overall strategy. By-the-way, you won't get that kind of service from a robo-advisor. In those automated investment systems, you are just someone tapping a link on a computer screen. Someone needs to talk to you about your goals and dreams, and how they affect your taxes.

Alot of what I do involves solving complicated math problems—but this is not math for the masses. These are the numbers that reflect your individual needs, goals and situation. Working together, we can discover what adds up to the right strategies for you and your family involving taxes and the many other elements of comprehensive financial planning.

CHAPTER 8

Health Wise

In our part of the country, as in many other areas, just about everybody knows somebody who has lost a family farm or family business because it had to be sold to pay for a loved one's nursing-home care. Too often, legacies are lost because of a lack of planning. It is not an uncommon situation, and it is now exacerbated by the fact that folks are living longer than ever before.

I have noticed, however, that many people only get motivated to do such planning when they see what has happened to someone else—usually someone they know who is about their same age. They may start to panic, since often they are in their sixties or seventies and may possibly be no longer insurable for long-term care. When folks in that situation come to me, I listen carefully and offer to do whatever I can. But I cannot work miracles. Often, by the time their situation has become very real to them, unfortunately it is may be too late.

My father purchased long-term care insurance years ago. A lifelong successful farmer and insurance professional, he took that action to make sure that the legacy of his years of hard work would be passed on to his sons. I admire his example. I believe you don't do long-term care planning solely for yourself. You do it for your heirs. You do it for the next generation, to protect their legacy. You also do it to ease their minds knowing that resources will be available to help take care of you.

It has only been recently that my father has needed the kind of care that his policy covers. Fortunately, he is as sharp as he ever has been. We can sit and talk business and sports or about the kids or whatever. But at age eighty-five, his diabetes and past bouts with cancer have taken a toll on his health. It's hard to accept that one of your parents is in a nursing home and will probably never leave. But long ago, he anticipated a day might come when he and our family would need to employ specialized help to care for him. I deeply respect his foresight in providing for himself and in protecting his legacy for my brothers and me.

In this chapter, we will take a look at the various options available for protecting yourself from the financial risk of an extended period of long-term disability in old age.

Traditional long-term care insurance

Traditional long-term care insurance is the route that many people have taken over the years. The primary goal with this type of protection is to provide assets for your family to help take care of you and to protect against the catastrophic costs. For most families, the most important things to protect against are the ongoing expenses that could financially drain you, or your family and heirs, if you should need to go into a long-term care facility. I have found that the clients who are usually most interested in long-term care coverage often have, or have had, parents in a facility. They clearly understand how potentially devastating those costs can be for a family.

But know that this type of protection is an investment in your family's legacy. Long-term care coverage can be expensive. Some people object to traditional insurance because of its "use it or lose it" nature. They are wary of paying those premiums for all those years for a benefit that they may never utilize. I get that. They are concerned about wasting their money—although what they are buying is not necessarily the care itself, but the peace of mind in case it is needed. That's the premise of all insurance.

As part of our planning conversation with clients, I will often ask what steps they have taken, or wish to take, to protect against the possibility of needing a prolonged period of long-term care. More than once, I have heard this response in jest: "I've told the kids to just take me out back and shoot me. I'm not going to be a burden to anyone!"

"I'll bet about anything that the kids aren't going to shoot you!" I tell them. "They love you, and they'll do what they can to help, but I'm pretty sure they won't shoot you. So what's your Plan B?"

And sometimes clients tell me that they will just let the state take care of them. Yes, this may be an option through Medicaid, but many people don't realize that the state, or Medicaid, will only step in after you have done everything you can to provide for yourself. And yes, this may mean selling the bulk of your potential legacy.

Still, some people may resist the idea of having to spend down most of their assets before becoming eligible for Medicaid. They would prefer, it seems, to keep their wealth while passing off the responsibility to the taxpayers. And I get that too. No one wants to see their life's work and savings get eaten up by the expense of staying in a care facility. But as a fellow taxpayer, I think that you will agree that it is only right for people to pay their own way as much as possible before turning to the government for support. I often suggest to people that they consider some method of long-term care protection so that they will not be in that situation.

Before the government will step in, it requires that you take care of yourself as long as you can. Title 19, the acronym for this section of the tax code, is a necessary program. Some people do need assistance, but I believe the government should step in only when it must. That is why you cannot become eligible for Medicaid coverage of nursing-home care until you have spent down the majority of your own assets.

Sometimes people tell me that it looks as if their mother or father will be going into a nursing home and ask me how they can get assets out of their parents' name to protect them. I explain that there are ways to do that, such as through transfer of titles and gifting. However, I point out to them that if their mother or father needs to enter a nursing home within five years, the government could withhold benefits equivalent to the amount that was moved out of the parents' name. The government practices a five-year look back in which it searches for any attempt to hide or transfer assets. Most people are aware of that, but they may fail to act in time.

The lesson here is that if you are going to try to make mom or dad impoverished on paper, you have to do so at least five years in advance. At that stage, I often find that most parents are not ready to hand over the keys to the kingdom just yet. They are still using their hard-earned assets.

My father, for example, would never have wanted to have just given away his assets five years ago. He was feeling good, still in reasonable health, still wintering in Texas, and enjoying working in his woodshop. He did not anticipate needing help within five years, and yet that time did indeed come. I am forever grateful to him that he arranged so long ago to provide the necessary resources. Whether the state should become involved was never an issue. We all knew that he had done the right thing.

Alternatives for care

Some people, rather than purchase a long-term care policy, choose to self-insure. This is an option if you have sufficient resources, but because of the escalating costs associated with this type of care, it is not a fit for everyone.

In addition, you could choose asset-based alternatives that provide long-term care coverage. Annuity-based options have come onto the scene in the last few years, as well as life insurance policies containing a long-term care rider. We have been seeing a lot of interest in this approach over the last few years. This type of option works like this: you put a lump sum into the policy, and it guarantees you a long-term care benefit of a specific amount for a specific period. If you don't use it for long-term care, the amount of money in the policy will be leveraged as a life insurance benefit for your heirs. A lot of people like that arrangement because it avoids the "use it or lose it" scenario. No matter what, someone will receive benefits from the investment made into the contract.

I prefer to call it "extended care" or "long-term disability care for the elderly" rather than long-term care. The latter term, for some reason, tends to make people think exclusively about nursing homes.

Today there are many options available, particularly with advances in health care. Extended care could be assisted living. It could be adult daycare. It could be any of a number of semi-independent living arrangements with different levels and degrees of care. The traditional nursing home is far from being the only alternative available.

In fact, often we see children help their parents stay out of the nursing home as long as possible. They can help do this if they have the resources and ability to do so. Careful, advanced planning can help to assure that this will be the case. It is not always possible, but most people would prefer to stay in their own homes until the level of care they need makes that impossible. With today's alternatives, much can be done toward that end.

A crucial conversation

Current data suggests that about a third of us will either need long-term care or will have a loved one who will need it at some point in time.

When I speak to groups and ask how many in the audience know somebody in an extended-care facility, they virtually all raise their hands. But when I ask the next question—"How many think that person will someday be you?"—nobody raises a hand. "Well, I hate to break it to you," I say, "but look at the person on your left and the person on your right. Either you or one of them is likely to need long-term care. So do you have a plan?"

I understand that it's hard to think about. It's not comfortable to consider a time when you will be frail and unable to care for yourself.

However, it is essential to make sure that you take the right steps for your own sake, and for your children's sake, to provide the resources in case that situation arises.

As a CFP®, part of my fiduciary responsibility is to get you to look at the deepest and darkest sides of life. I need to help you consider what would happen if you were to get sick or if you were to die prematurely. What if your spouse got sick or died? Your kids? This hardly makes for happy conversation, but we need to look at those type of possibilities. Otherwise, most folks would never take the steps needed to plan for the "what ifs" of life.

Most everyone understands why this type of planning is necessary, and they know that if left to their own devices, that kind of frank talk might never take place. "Don't worry," I always tell them with a smile, "Even though I may kill you off in my examples of what could happen, I will always bring you back before we are through!"

Ever-rising medical costs

Certainly your medical expenses will increase as you get older. That is part of the special inflation rate calculated for retirees. Medical expenses usually hit older individuals to a much greater degree than they do younger people. The risks associated with longevity include not only extended care expenses, but also the higher cost of medical care in general. Older folks tend to need more of it, and the costs are rising faster than for most other items we consume. That is one reason I recommend that our clients figure their living expenses during retirement at close to what they were during their working years. They may be spending less on some things, but much more on areas such as healthcare.

Navigating through the options for health care and prescription drug coverage during retirement can be quite confusing. There are numerous plans and supplements to consider. It is beyond the scope of this book to explain it all, but let me reassure you that most retirees need assistance to find what works best for them. Help is readily available for those who would need guidance to take them through these steps.

CHAPTER 9
Building Income to Last

Denise and I were in college when we began dating, and neither of us had a spare dime. When our relationship started to get more serious, I figured that at least some of our conversation should be about the future. I wanted her to know that I was the kind of guy who would be attentive to our financial security. I was, after all, minoring in business.

"So, when it comes to your money, do you keep a budget or anything?" I asked her one day. I don't remember what led up to this conversation, but somehow it came up. Perhaps it was my timing, but she seemed puzzled. I tried to explain in more technical terms: "I mean, what I am trying to say is—how do you know how much money to spend on food and stuff?"

"Well," she said, after pausing thoughtfully, "when I run out of money, I just eat popcorn."

I was in love, and her response made her no less adorable in my eyes. At least she had thought it through, I figured. I knew she was the one for me. However, I must say that the popcorn approach to income planning is not one that I recommend today to my clients. I believe that they deserve a lifestyle that provides for a higher quality of diet!

Income planning for retirement is the crux of our practice. Our primary focus is on helping people position their assets and make the right decisions so that they can sleep well at night. It's one thing to reminisce with a chuckle about those shoestring college days. It's quite another to anticipate with anxiety the possibility of a shoestring retirement.

In previous chapters we have examined the changing nature of retirement planning. All of the areas covered in this book are inter-related. They all, in one way or another, may have a direct, or indirect effect on your retirement income. No part of one's financial picture can be looked at in a vacuum. This includes all of the various income sources as well.

Besides the income that they may be anticipating from a pension and/or from Social Security, most folks will also need a personal portfolio to supplement their cash flow. Fortunately, there are a variety of options to utilize when designing a plan. A plan to help see them all the way through a comfortable retirement.

The details of such a plan may vary considerably from client to client. But generally they will have this in common: the portfolio will need to include what we call "spend-now money," which needs to be readily available for immediate expenses; "spend-later money," which will become available at various times in the future; and for many it may include "never-spend money," which will be left for their heirs or charity.

We believe in positioning our clients' resources in what you might think of as a series of buckets, each with its own specific purpose. Since you will be using the money in different ways, we believe you should not treat it all the same. In other words, you may need to invest in a variety of different asset classes and/or types that work in accordance with your overall retirement-income plan. When designing this approach, we look closely at the expenses, costs, and tax implications—and at how the expected returns and risk of each investment work in conjunction with your other retirement income streams.

One primary goal is to ensure that your portfolio will be able to keep pace with inflation and meet your long-term objectives.

Once you reach retirement age and potentially start spending down your nest egg, you cannot become so conservative with it that you sidestep all potential for growth. We coach our clients to continue to take a somewhat long-term perspective, even during retirement. It can be hard to think that way when you are counting the eggs in your basket and wanting to keep them secure. Just remember that you and your spouse will likely still have decades ahead of you.

But retirement planning does not end on your final day of work. It continues until your final day on earth, and even beyond, if you need to make sure and provide for someone else as well. If you allow yourself to become so conservative that your assets are just standing still, you may actually be losing ground over the course of those years as your purchasing power diminishes. Think once again about how much more it costs to replace those car tires these days. That's why you need to keep that long-term perspective. That's why your money needs to continue to have an opportunity for growth. To maintain its' purchasing power.

Resources and the bucket system

Not every investment vehicle, of course, is going to satisfy your growth objective for the long term. Nor will every investment provide you with the level of safety you are seeking for the short term. Your overall strategy needs to be a balance of safety, growth, and liquidity.

To achieve higher long-term growth potential, you may need to take a higher degree of risk with part of your resources, and you may need to give up immediate access to a portion of those funds for a period of time. If you need liquidity, such as for your immediate expenses, and you desire a higher degree of principal safety, then you need to accept that the return on those funds is likely to be relatively lower. Different investments are utilized for different needs. Different buckets for different purposes. That is the basic premise of the multiple-bucket income-planning strategy.

We believe establishing an emergency fund is a good place to start. Even though that's not a bucket that you are going to rely on for income, you will still need it. Life happens to all of us. Cars break down, furnaces go out, and kids get sick. Without an emergency fund for these types of contingencies, you most likely will find yourself forced to dip into your other "buckets"—the ones that are designed for your future income needs.

The next bucket that you may need to set up will take care of your short-term income needs. This will include your day-to-day money for living expenses. A number of factors, including your goals and your age, will play into your investment decisions here. We might consider a combination of mutual funds or advisory accounts, or investments that are growth-oriented and yet liquid. They are designed so that you can get to them as your income needs arise. Proceeds from these assets often can be transferred to your checking or savings account for easy access and use.

Looking out further into your future, we might utilize tools such as annuities or advisory accounts with a longer-term perspective to generate buckets of income that will keep pace with inflation. Each of these buckets is used in combination with the others, and you draw upon them at the appropriate times. The goal is to position resources to be there to serve your short-term, midterm, and long-term needs. Your longer-term buckets in effect will replenish your shorter-term ones.

Some clients may also want to have a "never-need bucket." They have resources that they know they may never spend. When that is the case, our goal is to treat that money in the most efficient manner for passing it on to their heirs or charity. (Remember the IRA/RMD arbitrage strategy?) Though it is not directly part of income planning, because it will never become spending money, it still must be set aside to be invested appropriately for that purpose. In that way, it becomes part of their bucket system. It is part of their overall plan.

In most cases, these buckets may represent separate accounts. Sometimes, we might have an advisory account that is structured for both the medium and the long term, but in general, these are separate account types. We might suggest that the client keep the emergency fund in a savings account at his or her local bank. Safety, not growth potential, is the goal with this account. It is usually best will to keep these assets easily accessible and safe. They may ask us to handle that portion of their money, but usually it is more advantageous for clients to keep it at their local bank or credit union.

Then, for an account that is designated to feed the immediate-income bucket, we often look at several different options. There are options such as a fixed-index annuity with a five- or ten-year payout, or even a single premium immediate annuity (SPIA) for a short, five-year period. Or perhaps a bond or CD ladder is the right fit.

Depending on the needs of each client, often we will use a combination of strategies. You may be able to leverage certain accounts and have them spend down over five or ten years, which will allow other buckets with riders and benefits on them to grow. That could provide a certain guaranteed income level in ten years or more. Meanwhile, you may have another growing bucket, such as an advisory account that is designed to keep pace with inflation. In other words, you turn on different streams of income at different times. That is how an "Asset Cycle Portfolio" system works (Asset Cycle Portfolio is a Registered Trademark of USA Financial).

We do have some folks who prefer a simple system of regular and established withdrawals from their portfolio. Basically, with this system, they have one or two accounts that are set up to maintain a withdrawal strategy. We are happy to design these types of income strategies as well. However, we have found that the bucket system is often more useful when part of the goal is to create guaranteed income streams for certain goals, or periods, of their retirement. We interview our clients to find out which direction would be best for them and which method they would prefer.

With retirement-income planning, eventually the rising cost of living may become an issue. Therefore, we often will build in another bucket that will provide a "raise," so to speak, to combat inflation. The further into the future we are looking, the more growth we can anticipate. Since that portion of your money will not be needed for quite some time, it can be invested somewhat more aggressively—

similar to the way you could invest more aggressively when you were younger. The last buckets tend to be more traditional brokerage or advisory accounts that are invested with a long-term perspective, with no immediate planned withdrawals. These are designed to provide the raises and protection against inflation that are needed. All of this is built into the system from the beginning as we try to take your income concerns off the table.

It basically comes down to this idea: You may not want to take much risk on money that you will need immediately or for emergencies. These resources must be there for you in the short term. Down the road, you may want to accept more risk so your money can grow; otherwise, inflation will take its toll. But since you are not planning to touch that money for a while, you have time on your side. Even if your account dips due to short-term volatility, hopefully it will have plenty of time to recover and grow anew.

Of course, within all of these buckets, we consider the potential tax consequences; we look at required minimum distribution requirements if applicable, and we look at how each bucket will interact with the different Social Security strategies. When we put together these buckets, we do so in conjunction with all the other factors of your financial plan and in consideration of all of your other income streams.

The major factor that governs how the buckets are designed is what our clients want out of life—their objectives for a successful retirement. Sometimes adjustments have to be made if available resources simply are insufficient to do what the client wants. In that case, we look for compromises. If the resources cannot supply an income stream to meet basic needs, we may have to use tools that rely somewhat more on future market performance.

First, however, we try to use tools that will limit the client's risk profile as much as possible. Since the goal is to eliminate worry, we look to design strategies with known income streams if possible. We look for strategies with the least amount of risk that still have the potential to accomplish the stated objectives.

Earlier in this book, we took a look at sequence-of-return risk. This risk demonstrates what can happen to your portfolio if you are invested entirely in the market and it falls, or has a few down years, just as you are retiring and taking money from your portfolio. To a large extent, the bucket system can help address that potential disaster. With this strategy, you are not drawing from an account that is fully at the mercy of the markets for your current income. You get your income from more secure sources, which gives you the ability to keep your hands off the money that you have set aside for growth.

We may not be able to eliminate all sequence-of-return risk, but how close we can come will depend upon what we learn about you, your goals, and your dreams. We strive to determine how that may translate into dollars. What do you need to make life good for you and your family? How much income do you need to do the things you wish to do? Now, and in the future?

When you get right down to it, most people are less concerned about how much money they will have in the end than they are about whether they will have enough along the way to do the things they want to do. They want that sense of security, knowing that their money will be there for them. They don't want to worry about waking up in the morning and hearing on the news that the market has fallen. They want to live a life free of the prospect of panic. It is our goal to help you arrange your finances that way. To the degree that it is possible, we help our clients do just that.

GPS for Retirement

Retirement-income planning is the core of what we provide for our clients. It is far different from the type of investment planning done during one's working and accumulation years. For decades to come, what you have gathered needs to continue providing for you and your family. This is a huge responsibility, and you need guidance from someone who is in tune with your needs at this stage of life. There are no "mulligans" or "do-overs." This has to be done correctly the first time. Together we work to make this happen.

In this era when pensions are fading away, you may need to replace that missing leg of the stool. That's where annuities may sometimes play a useful role in retirement-income planning. A pension, after all, is simply a form of annuity payout. Beyond that, however, we are looking at your entire retirement picture and finding the right tools that will work best in each situation that you may encounter.

In drafting a retirement-income plan, most people are seeking confidence. They are designing a system in which the money will be coming in as long as they live. You want to know that you will to be able to provide for your family's needs. If you have sufficient resources, you may even be considering your financial legacy for future generations.

"Make sure your outflows do not exceed your inflows, or your upkeep will be your downfall," James Norris, my mentor from whom we bought our practice, was fond of saying

It was his version of an old saying that is profound in its simplicity. Don't spend more than you bring in, or eventually, you will run out of money. We work to utilize multiple-bucket planning and other tools to help make it all work, but that saying captures the essence of retirement-income planning.

CHAPTER 10

The Right Tools for the Job

Growing up on the farm as the youngest of three sons, I was often relegated to the job of "go-for." And I don't mean the furry kind that digs up your yard! When my Dad and brothers were working on something and they needed a particular wrench, or screw, or whatever, because I was the youngest, I was always the one sent to "go-get-it" or the one that would "go-for" this or "go-get that!" So, because I was a kid, I used to argue sometimes and ask them, "Why can't you just use what you have? Why can't you just make it work?"

To this day, I can still remember my dad telling me that sometimes, we can just make it work. But, sometimes it takes a certain tool to perform a certain task. And sometimes, even if a job can be done utilizing different tools, there may be one or two certain "specialty designed" tools that make performing that task easier and much more efficient!

This wisdom is something that we strive to implement in our retirement income and financial planning with our clients. Matching the right financial tool to the task we need to do. All too often in our industry we see advisors who try to force all of their clients into one or two types of strategies or investments. Sort of a "one-size-fits-all" mentality. And this may happen for a variety of reasons.

Sometimes the advisor is only able to sell certain type of investments or strategies because they are captive to their firm and only have a few investments they can use. Sometimes it is because they are only licensed to use a limited number of products, such as insurance-based products only. Sometimes it is because they have a limited knowledge base and do not fully understand the different types of investment and planning tools that are available. And unfortunately, sometimes they only recommend a certain product because that is the one that will do the best for *them* financially, not necessarily the client.

Independence and choice

One of the greatest advantages of working as an independent financial planner in a privately owned firm is that we have access to a vast array of financial "tools" and strategies. We are not beholden to anyone. We do not have to utilize any certain investment or accounts or have to meet any type of company quotas. Because of this freedom to use what is in the best interest of our clients, we can utilize the financial tools that are the most efficient depending upon each client's particular situation and objectives. In other words, we know we can drive a nail into a wall with the socket wrench, but a hammer sure works better! So we say, let's use the right tool.

When building our retirement-income plans utilizing a "multiple-bucket" strategy, we have the ability to match up the most efficient asset type with the objective for that particular bucket. By being able to use different asset types and allocations, we can also allocate for risk tolerance at the same time. In addition, because we understand the different tax treatment of each type of investment, we can also incorporate that planning consideration into the plan as well.

Another advantage we have as an independent firm is the opportunity to associate with several different types of entities for our inventory of financial tools that we use. This provides us access to product brokers and firms that may specialize in certain planning areas or product types. This added advantage helps provide us with access to product-knowledge professionals to help us when designing specific strategies for our clients.

The following is a list of the types of strategies that we offer in our firm and may use with our clients as part of their investment, retirement income, financial estate, or other type of planning. The type of strategies we utilize for each planning situation is unique to their situation and is dependent upon the individual needs of the client.

Strategies Offered:

- Retirement-income plans**
- Customized financial plans*
- Account-aggregation platforms**
- Social Security planning strategies*
- Small business retirement plans**
- Financial Estate-planning strategies*
- IRAs*
- Variable annuities*

- Fixed and indexed annuities**
- Fee-based advisory accounts*
- Brokerage accounts*
- Exchange-traded funds*
- Stocks & bonds*
- REITS* (Real Estate Investment Trusts)
- Mutual funds*
- Small business retirement plans*
- Company-sponsored qualified savings plans 401(k), 403(b), etc.*
- Life insurance**
- Disability insurance**
- Long-term care planning**
- Medicare supplement plans**
- Medicare Part D/Advantage Plans**
- Company-sponsored group health plans**
- Individual health insurance plans**

**Distributed through Miller Financial Group

Putting it in context

So which "financial tools" are right for you and your family? There is no way to know unless you utilize the strategy in the right context. Each one of the strategies listed may be right for you, or they may be completely wrong. It all depends upon your situation and what you wish to accomplish.

We often hear some people say that they would never use a certain type of product, investment, or strategy. For example, let's say someone makes the comment that they will never buy an annuity because they claim they all have high expenses, are illiquid, and confusing. Are they? I think it all depends on what you are trying to accomplish and what you are comparing it to. If your goal is to purely grow your assets and that is it, they may not be the asset of choice. But, if your goal is tax-deferred growth and the ability to create income that you may not be able to outlive, and that is a critical need in your retirement-income plan, it may not be so "expensive" or "confusing" after all. Every investment has to be looked at in context with how it is intended to be used. Plus you need to work with someone who understand how they work and if it fits your particular situation.

To illustrate this, let's use nitroglycerin as an example. When many people hear this term, they think of using it as an explosive and blowing something up. On the other hand, some people may think of how it is used in medicine as a method to treat coronary heart disease. Two totally different uses for the same "tool." Both answers are correct when put in the right context and used in the correct manner based upon what they are trying to accomplish.

This is what we strive to do when utilizing the various financial strategies and tools in our financial tool box. No one investment or strategy is going to be right for everyone in all situations. Our goal is to find the right tools for the job.

CHAPTER 11

An Enduring Legacy

I once sat down with a new client to review his financial-planning documents and made an unusual discovery. We were going over his life insurance contracts, and I noticed that his beneficiary was someone whom he had yet to mention in our conversations.

"Bob, who is this person?" I asked him, pointing to the designation page. "Who is this lady here?"

"Cynthia? Oh, she's my ex-wife. But as you know, I remarried. My wife now is Donna."

"Do you realize, Bob, that if you were to pass away, this policy would pay out to Cynthia, not to Donna?"

"Oh that's not an issue," he told me. "See, I had my will redone, and we had Cynthia stricken from everything . . ."

I interrupted him. "Bob, I hate to tell you this, but the life insurance company doesn't really care about that, and neither would a judge. All that matters is who you have listed here as the beneficiary.

This serves as a contractual agreement between you and the insurance company. And contract law will supersede any directions in a will or trust."

His jaw dropped. "Oh my God. We've got to take care of that today," he said. It was a $1 million life insurance policy. I am sure his ex-wife would have been happy to have received that death benefit someday.

From that point forward, he was among one of my most loyal clients. I find it very satisfying to be of such service, but frankly, I wish that never had to be the case. I feel one of the most important things I can do for my clients is point out to each and every client how essential it is that we conduct that beneficiary-designation review. These are contractual agreements between you and your 401(k) provider, the life insurance company, or whomever you are dealing with. Make no mistake: those designations will take precedence over directions in a will or a trust if either is ever challenged in court.

Even though you may assume that all is well, I would encourage you to review these documents again: It may have been years since you listed your beneficiaries. In your family, children may have been born and people may have died, and perhaps you or another family member divorced. Double checking and updating those designations might not be top of mind for you as you go about your everyday life. Nonetheless, you should do it regularly, please! This is particularly crucial for blended families in which one spouse, or both, have children from a previous marriage. Without an update, you could inadvertently disinherit somebody and/or let an ex-spouse or other family member claim your resources.

You should consult with a qualified financial planner and with an estate-planning attorney. Most people prefer not to think about their own mortality, and so they may tend to put these matters on the back burner. Estate planning deals with one's death, which can be difficult to contemplate. Nonetheless, you must do it. It's part of being a responsible adult. Life changes. Life ends. There is a lot to do in the meantime. It needs to be done right, and it needs to be done soon!

The big perspective

As part of the planning process, we help a lot of folks with their estate planning. I am not an attorney, but as a CFP®, I do help to coordinate a lot of decision making on how to best handle their estates. I feel it is my responsibility to help our clients properly position their legacy.

As a fiduciary, I take that responsibility very seriously. Making sure that our clients have set up their beneficiary designations correctly is just one aspect of estate planning—although we call it "the first line of defense." It also may involve searching for ways to ensure that their assets will grow in the most tax-efficient manner. Estate planning also may involve helping them to find an attorney to handle the more technical aspects.

Until they are under fire, people often do not take the time to learn about proper estate planning. Perhaps a parent passes away, and all of a sudden they have to figure it all out. That's not the ideal time, to say the least. People who have gone through that ordeal tend to become more diligent about their own estate planning. But sometimes it's too late to have helped their parents or a sibling or a spouse.

I believe no one aspect of financial planning should be managed without considering all the other aspects.

Each part will affect the others. When you see your doctor he doesn't just prescribe a pill or make a recommendation without considering how that diagnosis and prescription may affect the rest of your overall health. The same is true when looking at all of the parts of one's financial life. The plan is, in effect, a guide for living, and human beings are complex creatures. Our dreams influence our actions, and our actions influence our dreams. Estate and legacy planning is one of those integral elements of retirement planning.

As I mentioned previously, here in rural America, agriculture has long been central to the lives and fortunes of a great many families. Often these families may have several children, and it is common that only one or two of the siblings are interested in taking over the family-farming business. The others may have little or no interest at all in that pursuit.

What, then, can be done so that each of the children is treated in a manner that you consider fair? Are there resources available to equalize the estate? Whether you will be able to efficiently plan for that transition may depend, in large part, on the decisions and actions you have taken regarding other aspects of your financial plan. It all interrelates. We believe you must consider the big picture as it relates to financial and estate planning.

The basic elements

Whether we know it or not, every one of us has an estate plan. But it might not be one that we have prepared with the help of an estate planning attorney and our financial planner. It might be your state government's default plan, and you might not like the state's plan as much as one that you would design yourself with the help of professional counsel.

Most estate plans should include some basic elements. Most will include a will, powers of attorney, trusts if they are needed, and a living will and/or a medical directive. Beyond that, it can be as complex as your estate-planning needs require. That complexity will be dictated by your family situation, your desires for leaving a legacy, the extent of your wealth, the number of people in your family, and other factors.

We usually recommend that families at least put together a simple will. Informally, we call it the "I love you" will because generally it is between a husband and wife and simply directs that if something happens to one, everything goes to the other spouse. The will also names executors, as well as contingent executors and trustees. The will needed for your specific situation may also include other instructions and requirements. These may include items such as a testamentary trust to care for minor children or specific bequests of property.

You will also want to provide two powers of attorney—one for general financial affairs, so that someone will be able to pay your bills and handle your business affairs if you become incapacitated, and the other specifically for medical decision making. Also, a living will is important if you wish to direct clinicians on the extent to which they should attempt to resuscitate you if necessary.

A HIPAA (Health Insurance Portability and Accountability Act of 1996) release is another important document. Often, when I ask folks when they last reviewed their will, they tell me that it has been ten or fifteen years. "Do you know if you have an up-to-date HIPAA release on file?" I ask, and they seldom know what I mean. Without that document, your doctor or the hospital may not be authorized to release your medical information to those who are trying to help make decisions for you. If you are hurt, or become very ill and unable to make decisions for yourself, this document can be critical.

If you desire to keep the passing of your estate private, a trust may be a good tool for you to consider. In working with our clients, we discuss the difference between revocable and irrevocable trusts, and where they may, or may not fit. "Irrevocable" means precisely that—you cannot change it, and so if you wish to utilize such a trust, you need to be ready to release control. However, it is also a highly valuable means by which you may be able to move assets out of your estate for tax purposes.

The term "Revocable Trust" means just what it says. The terms of the trust can be changed, or "revoked" by the trustees. This type of trust can be undone and dissolved if needed. One of the primary uses of this type of trust is to act as a "will-substitute" and allow assets to pass to the next generation outside of the probate process. But because these trusts can be changed, or "revoked," assets held in this type of trust are still considered to be part of one's estate at their passing.

We also review the beneficiary designations, as we mentioned previously, along with the proper titling of their assets. How certain assets are titled will also take precedence over the wording in a will or trust. We also go through the concepts of joint tenants with rights to survivorship and tenants in common, etc. We don't have to worry about common law here in Iowa, but we do work in other states that utilize that titling option. We make sure that folks understand the differences and recommend that they consult with an attorney when deciding how to properly title their property.

Passing to family and charity

If you have resources that you will not be using in your lifetime and you have philanthropic desires, we help you look for ways to maximize the efficiency of those assets. We look at how you may be able to pass assets to your favorite charities, just as we would look for efficient ways to pass money to your heirs.

There are many strategies and tools for philanthropic planning. It is very important to work with a specialist on setting up the details of these strategies. But, I do go over the general concepts with clients, and we talk about the possibilities. We may look at such strategies as utilizing a charitable-remainder trust and/or charitable funds that can help to simplify the investment and decision making. We also may look at the advantages of using life insurance as a charitable and estate-leveraging tool. In most cases, the proceeds from life insurance policies pass on to beneficiaries tax-free. Life insurance can also be a useful tool for equalizing an estate—such as providing a benefit for those children who don't want to take over the family business.

We do a lot of business-transition planning with small businesses of all kinds. I come from a commercial-lending and entrepreneurial background. I understand the issues involved in selling a business or transitioning it to the next generation, whether it's a farm, a dental practice, or a microbrewery—all of which are types of businesses that I have assisted with their business transition planning.

Let's say a daughter wants to take over her family's insurance business, but she will need to buy out two or three siblings who have an interest in the realizing some value out of the business, but not in operating it. The premium on a life insurance policy is usually small compared with the benefit of the lump sum it may generate upon the parents' passing. The leveraging opportunity is often ten to one or more. It may make perfect sense to prefund the buyout of the other heirs, utilizing a life insurance policy. They want and deserve their share. Simply because they are not interested in the business does not mean that they have no stake in the family wealth. Life insurance, properly positioned, may help transition a business to the next generation without saddling the successor with excess debt. It may also help allow the business to stay in the family.

Businesses of all sorts represent a way of life that bridges generations. Through thoughtful and careful estate planning, that way of life may be able to be preserved. However, unless these issues are dealt with effectively, families can become splintered. Businesses can be forced to shut down. With the boom in farmland values, for example, this is a particularly big risk in our part of the country. Farming is big business today. It is a tragedy when I see a lack of proper planning result in a family fighting over the value and money in an estate.

Estate planning is about much more than money. It's about leaving a legacy. It's about values and ethics. It's about who you were and what you believed in. That is what you are leaving behind, and it is every bit as important as the money. Your legacy is the mark that you leave on the world.

Daniel S. Miller is not an attorney. For advice relating to your specific situation, please consult a qualified estate planning attorney.

CONCLUSION
Stewards and Caretakers

I have always admired the image of a cowboy leaning forward in the saddle. He pushes onward, no matter what. Through the rain, the mud, or the wind, he gets it done. He moves forward without complaint.

I believe we could all do well to follow that example. We should always be pushing forward with integrity. We should get the task done and do what's right. We are on this earth as caretakers. We should watch over this world and our fellow man, taking pride in who we are and the work we do. We should be true to our word, doing what we say we will do, looking one another in the eye. We should always be extending a helping hand. To me, that's what it means to be living a full life.

Growing up on the land and with the guidance of a good man as my father, I developed an appreciation of good stewardship. I enjoy working with people who have been good caretakers of their resources. I take it as a deep responsibility to take good care of the resources that others entrust to me.

I was raised with the spirit of caretaking and stewardship. These are the qualities instilled in me by my family from an early age. Each of us, including me, most certainly has room for improvement. But I know that I am on the right path. At every turn, I am trying to treat others as I would want to be treated—with dignity, honesty, and respect. I know that someone watches our every move and that we are writing our own legacy in all that we do, for better or for worse.

On our financial-planning folders that we present to our clients, we have printed these words: "The plans of the diligent lead to profit, as surely as haste leads to poverty." It is a Biblical truth preserved for all time in Proverbs 21:5. To me, that is the crux of everything we do. The way to thrive and prosper is to design a thoughtful and comprehensive plan and abide by it. It is simply the right thing to do.

EPILOGUE & FAQ

Where Do You Go From Here?

At this point, I want to "Thank you" for staying with me through this journey regarding what I, and our firm, feel is important when it comes to preparing for ones' financial life after their working years. Hopefully you can tell that this is an area that we are very passionate about. It is this passion for helping our clients and seeing the difference we can help make in their lives that drives everything we do as a firm.

No one in our industry, or any other financial discipline, has all of the answers. But the one thing I do believe we have, are the right questions to ask. The critical questions that pertains to your families' unique situation. Then, being able to assimilate the data and information into YOUR PLAN that addresses YOUR GOALS, and YOUR DESIRES. We believe that is the difference between working with a qualified retirement income planning professional, and those that just give it a good try.

So where do you go from here? We suggest you meet with us or someone who will help address some of those questions and concerns that you may have in the back of your mind. Those questions that maybe you think you might know the answers to, but aren't exactly sure. The questions that may make you a little uncomfortable, or make you feel uneasy about your future financial picture.

So what are these questions? Until we meet and get to know you we are not able to know exactly what questions we should ask and areas to address. But to give you a few examples, I have compiled the following list of General Frequently Asked Questions. I have compiled this to give you an idea of the types of issues and questions that you/we may wish to address as part of your financial and retirement income planning. Please note that this list is NOT ALL INCLUSIVE. This is only a small sampling of the type of general questions that may, or may not, apply to your situation. **These types of questions help lead a qualified planner to drill down deeper to address your particular financial situation.**

Frequently Asked General Questions: Examples

PRE-RETIREMENT:

- Am I setting aside enough in my retirement accounts now?
- How much can I afford to contribute now? What is the best type of account for me to utilize?
- How much difference can I still make in my retirement picture?

- Is there anything I can do to "catch-up" if I feel like I am behind at this point?
- Why do I want to retire? Am I ready for this major change in my day-to-day life?
- If I retire, how will I fill my days? Is my spouse on-board and ready for this change as well?
- Am I financially prepared? How do I know? Who do I look to for advice?
- How much income are we going to need?
- Have I sat down with a qualified retirement income planner? Do I have a plan designed to help my resources last as long as I do?
- What is retirement going to look like for me, and my spouse? Am I heading for the golf course, the easy chair, or starting a new business venture?
- Am I retiring for good, or just switching gears? Does making a change now make sense for me and my family?
- Where will I/we live in retirement? If moving, will our resources support our standard of living in this new local?

RETIREMENT:

- How do I handle my existing retirement accounts? What about my 401k or IRAs? How do I access income from each of these in the most tax-efficient manner?
- What about my non-qualified investment accounts or annuities? What are the tax implications of each account type?
- In what order should I draw down my assets to make sure they last and to be as tax efficient as possible?

- What about the beneficiaries on my accounts? Have these been updated? Have I had any changes in my family that could affect these?
- When should I take Social Security? How do I coordinate my benefits with the rest of my resources? With my spouse's benefits?
- Will I receive a pension? If so, how do I coordinate it with the rest of my retirement income sources? Does it contain spousal benefits to be considered?
- What about non-cash asset resources? Investment such as farmland or a business?
- How will these be utilized as part of the retirement income plan? Will I continue to receive income or will a portion be liquidated?
- How will the use or liquidation of my assets for retirement income affect our financial estate plan?
- What about life insurance at this point? How much is still needed, if any?
- Do I need to protect against my assets against long-term care expenses? If so, how do I do it?
- Who needs to be considered in my financial estate plan?

This list is just a sampling of the types of questions and issues we may address when we help our clients prepare for the next leg in their financial race. But remember this race is a marathon, not a sprint. Just as a runner prepares mentally for each part of a marathon, we believe you must prepare for each leg of your financial journey as well. So where do you go from here? If you have questions and would like some assistance along your financial journey, I and our team, would be glad to assist you. Thank you, Daniel S. Miller, CFP®

About the Author

Daniel S. Miller, CFP®, President,
Miller Financial Group, Inc.

Dan, a CERTIFIED FINANCIAL PLANNER™ professional, serves clients throughout the country as they transition toward retirement and work toward their financial goals. His firm's primary focus is to help make sure their clients will have the resources needed to provide and protect their income in retirement. Dan has almost twenty years' combined experience in the banking and financial services fields and has been with Miller Financial Group, Inc. (formerly Parker Norris Financial, Inc.) since 2004. Dan, along with his wife, Denise, purchased the firm in January 2013. Dan also works with business owners and agricultural professionals and has developed his own estate and succession-planning seminar for family-owned businesses and self-employed entrepreneurs. You can also tune in each Monday morning on 95.3 KCSI-FM, KOAK-AM Red Oak, IA, to hear Dan cohosting the firm's radio show, *Let's Talk Money!*

Dan and Denise are very proud of, and thankful for their team at Miller Financial Group, Inc. Without them, this book and how we assist our clients would not be possible. The team currently consists of Dan and Denise, Kaleb Robuck, Associate Advisor, Andrew Focht, Associate Advisor, Pat Przychodzin, Office Manager, Elizabeth Hyder, Marketing and Business Development Manager, Marian Hoffman, Health Insurance Specialist, Heather Huddle, Receptionist and Administrative Assistant, and Andrea Miller, Summer Intern and Office Assistant.

Dan's values of hard work and doing the right thing for his clients come from his roots of growing up on a diversified livestock and crop farm in Northwest Missouri. Growing up the youngest of three brothers, he learned that nothing comes easy and it takes hard work, perseverance, and treating people right to make a difference in the world.

Dan's qualifications and training include the following:

- CERTIFIED FINANCIAL PLANNER™ Professional
- Securities registrations: Series 6, 7, 63, 65
- Life, health, and disability insurance licensed
- College for Financial Planning, CFP® training
- Graduate of the Missouri School of Banking
- Bachelor of Science from Kansas State University in Animal Science with a Business minor

Daniel S. Miller is an investment adviser representative of, and securities and advisory services are offered through, USA Financial Securities Corp. (Member FINRA/SIPC). USA Financial Securities is a registered investment adviser located at 6020 E Fulton St., Ada, MI

49301. Miller Financial Group is not affiliated with USA Financial Securities.

Dan and his wife Denise live on an acreage just outside of Red Oak, IA, enjoying the wildlife and beauty provided by being a part of rural Iowa. Their son, Jackson, twenty-four, a graduate of the University of Northern Iowa, is now a graduate-level student at Iowa State University in Computer Engineering. Their daughter, Andrea, twenty-two, is a recent graduate of the University of Northern Iowa with a B.A. in Exercise Science in preparation for obtaining her doctorate in Occupational Therapy at Creighton University.

Dan and his family especially enjoy spending time with friends and family. Dan and Denise enjoy traveling, attending sporting events, and are big fans of the 2015 World Champion Kansas City Royals! They also enjoy hosting tailgate parties prior to watching their favorite football team, the 2015 NCAA Division II National Champions—the Northwest Missouri State Bearcats!

9 781599 326962